SCRABBLE™
CROSSWORD GAME BRAND

PUZZLES

VOLUME 2

Joe Edley

STERLING

New York / London
www.sterlingpublishing.com

2   4   6   8   10   9   7   5   3   1

Published by Sterling Publishing Co., Inc.
387 Park Avenue South, New York, NY 10016
© 2008 by Joe Edley
Distributed in Canada by Sterling Publishing
c/o Canadian Manda Group, 165 Dufferin Street,
Toronto, Ontario, Canada M6K 3H6

Sterling ISBN-13: 978-1-4027-5519-4
ISBN-10: 1-4027-5519-8

For information about custom editions, special sales, premium and
corporate purchases, please contact Sterling Special Sales
Department at 800-805-5489 or specialsales@sterlingpublishing.com.

Contents

Introduction

This book is for SCRABBLE fans who want to improve their game. After solving the hundreds of positions given, you will become a better player.

How Does This Book Work?

Each diagram shows you a mid-game position. Three racks accompany each diagram. For each rack your goal is to try to find the *highest-scoring play*. This play is not necessarily the "best" play in terms of what it opens up on the board for your opponent or what it leaves in your rack, but that's the play you're looking for. We've shown you how many points I was able to score with that rack in that position. In the unlikely event that you score more, you've outdone a three-time National SCRABBLE Champion and you should pat yourself on the back!

Each rack is independent of the others. So, once you've found a play with one rack, don't add that word to the board. Always begin each rack with the diagram just as it's shown on the page.

If you have trouble with a rack, consider the high-scoring hint and ask yourself how that can help lead you toward the answer. For example, if the score is more than 60 points, it's most likely a bingo (though not always!). If the score is divisible by three, perhaps it covers a Triple Word Score square.

Blanks on boards are indicated by outlined letters. In racks they appear as completely blank tiles. In the answers, letters that are formed from blank tiles are underlined.

I've tried to present several types of answers: Some are extensions of words already on the board, while others are words that cover two or more bonus squares in one turn. Some words are played parallel to words already on the board. For those parallel plays, also called overlapping plays, you'll want to refer to the word list on page 128. It lists all 101 two-letter words, as well as the three-letter words that can be formed from them. In general, forming parallel plays is one of the best ways to score more points. By learning the two-letter words, you'll have an edge on your opponents for finding those lucrative parallel plays during your own gameplay. So you can consider these puzzles as being practice for learning how to "read the board" in order to find your best plays.

All of the answer words are fairly common words, except possibly the two- and three-letter words. My advice is that if you find a word to play, but you're not sure whether the overlapping words are acceptable, then refer to word list. In doing so, by the time you're finished you'll have gone a long way toward learning those words and being able to form them without an aid in your own games. And, by the way, for language purists, all of the obscure two- and three-letter words shown in this book come from one of four popular collegiate American English dictionaries. I'm not making them up. Every word already on the board and every word formed in the answers are allowable words according to SCRABBLE tournament rules.

Hints

If you want further hints on any given rack, see page 121. The hints are placed after the answers so you can flip from the back without accidentally seeing any answers. The hints tell if an answer is an extension word, if it's a bingo, which bonus squares it covers, exactly how many letters it overlaps (if at least two), etc. That will go a long way toward helping you find the word! The puzzle's difficulty is indicated by stars, one star being the easiest, and four stars being the hardest.

Acknowledgments

I want to give a big thank-you to my editor, Peter Gordon, and former World and National SCRABBLE Champion Joel Sherman for their invaluable help in proofing these puzzles.

—Joe Edley

| | A | A | F | N | N | T | V | 32 | ★ |

| | D | G | I | L | N | O | T | 26 | ★ |

| | D | F | I | J | N | R | W | 28 | ★★ |

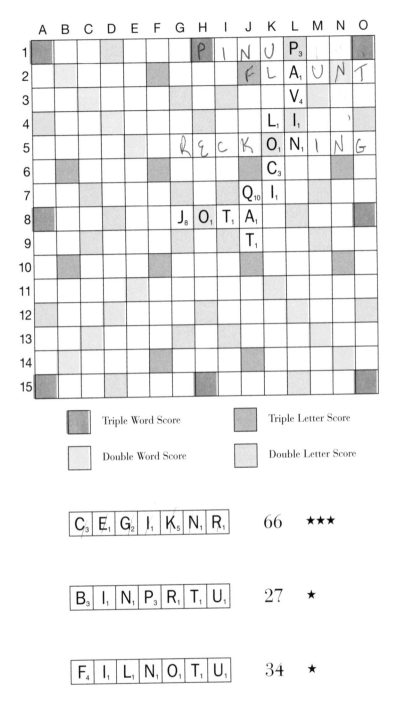

Triple Word Score   Triple Letter Score

Double Word Score   Double Letter Score

Adopt -- 14
Rapt = 18

A₁ D₂ I₁ I₁ P₃ T₁ U₁   26 ★

A₁ A₁ E₁ L₁ N₁ R₁ U₁   29 ★★

B₃ E₁ E₁ N₁ P₃ R₁ U₁   38 ★★

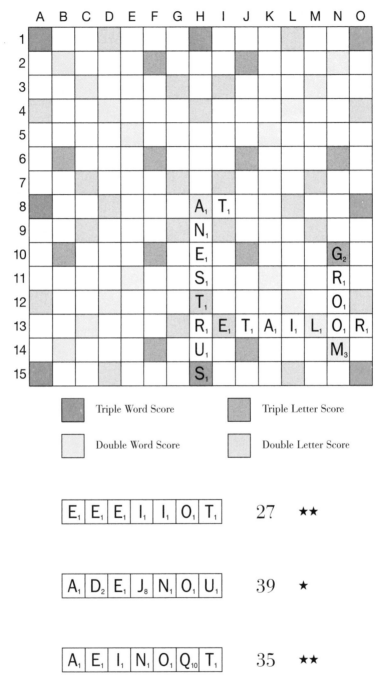

Triple Word Score | Triple Letter Score

Double Word Score | Double Letter Score

E₁ E₁ E₁ I₁ I₁ O₁ T₁   27   ★★

A₁ D₂ E₁ J₈ N₁ O₁ U₁   39   ★

A₁ E₁ I₁ N₁ O₁ Q₁₀ T₁   35   ★★

A₁ D₂ E₁ E₁ F₄ O₁ R₁   58   ★★

A₁ A₁ E₁ G₂ L₁ M₃ N₁   36   ★

D₂ G₂ L₁ M₃ N₁ T₁ W₄   43   ★★

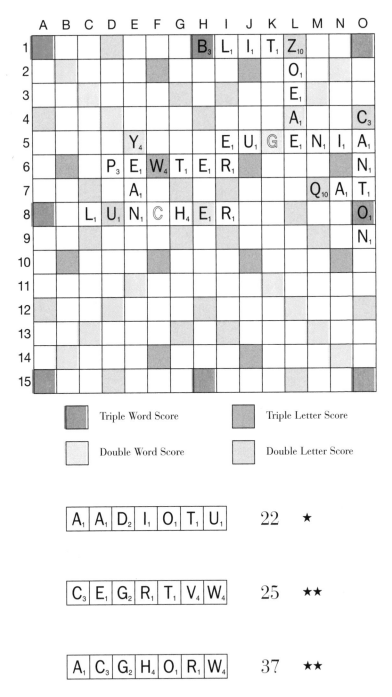

Triple Word Score

Triple Letter Score

Double Word Score

Double Letter Score

| B₃ | D₂ | H₄ | I₁ | L₁ | R₁ | Z₁₀ | 42 ★ |

| E₁ | F₄ | L₁ | M₃ | O₁ | R₁ | U₁ | 39 ★★ |

| A₁ | D₂ | E₁ | F₄ | O₁ | O₁ | P₃ | 48 ★★ |

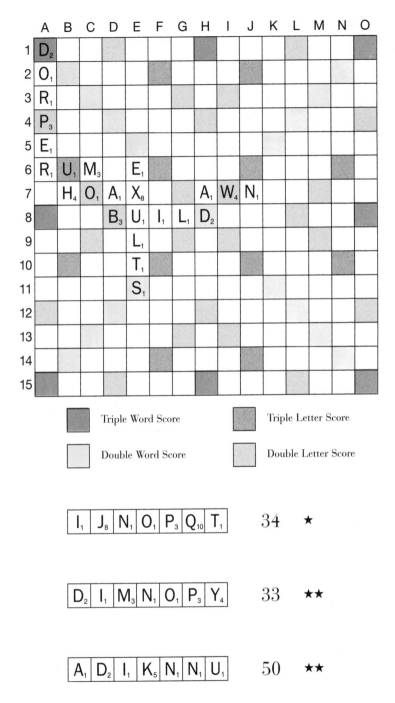

	A	B	C	D	E	F	G	H	I	J	K	L	M	N	O
1	D₂														
2	O₁														
3	R₁														
4	P₃														
5	E₁														
6	R₁	U₁	M₃		E₁										
7		H₄	O₁	A₁	X₈			A₁	W₄	N₁					
8				B₃	U₁	I₁	L₁	D₂							
9					L₁										
10					T₁										
11					S₁										
12															
13															
14															
15															

Triple Word Score   Triple Letter Score

Double Word Score   Double Letter Score

I₁ J₈ N₁ O₁ P₃ Q₁₀ T₁   34 ★

D₂ I₁ M₃ N₁ O₁ P₃ Y₄   33 ★★

A₁ D₂ I₁ K₅ N₁ N₁ U₁   50 ★★

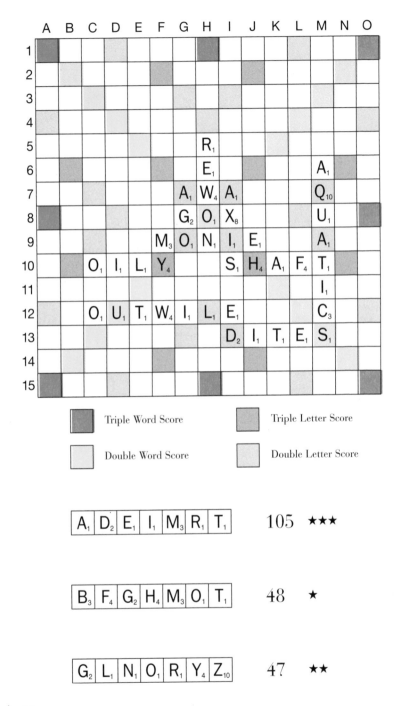

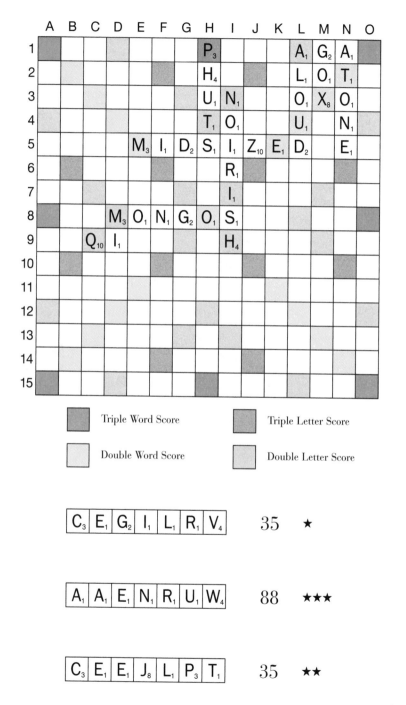

Triple Word Score   Triple Letter Score

Double Word Score   Double Letter Score

C₃ E₁ G₂ I₁ L₁ R₁ V₄   35   ★

A₁ A₁ E₁ N₁ R₁ U₁ W₄   88   ★★★

C₃ E₁ E₁ J₈ L₁ P₃ T₁   35   ★★

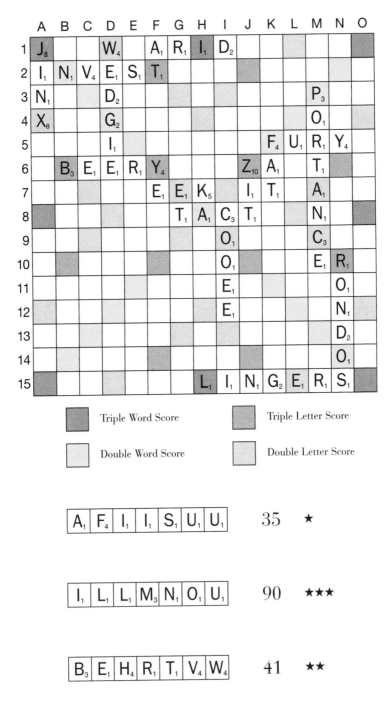

Triple Word Score

Triple Letter Score

Double Word Score

Double Letter Score

| A | F | I | I | S | U | U | 35 | ★ |

| I | L | L | M | N | O | U | 90 | ★★★ |

| B | E | H | R | T | V | W | 41 | ★★ |

D₂ H₄ I₁ L₁ N₁ O₁ R₁	34	★★	
D₂ D₂ E₁ I₁ M₃ T₁ U₁	30	★	
A₁ C₃ E₁ E₁ E₁ R₁ R₁	26	★★★	

Triple Word Score Triple Letter Score

Double Word Score Double Letter Score

A_1 B_3 G_2 L_1 N_1 O_1 U_1 29 ★★★

A_1 B_3 E_1 I_1 N_1 O_1 U_1 30 ★

A_1 E_1 F_4 N_1 P_3 R_1 W_4 43 ★★

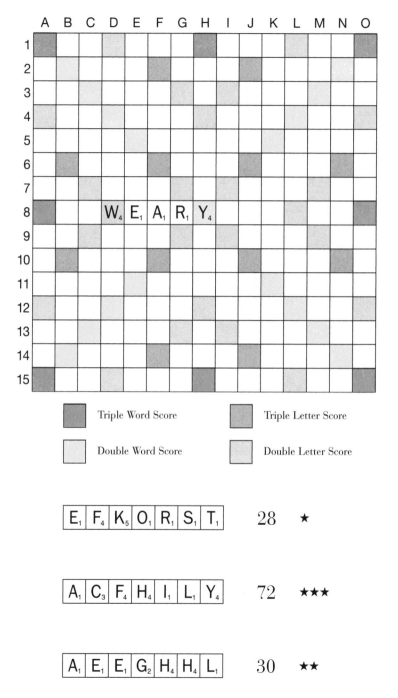

	A	B	C	D	E	F	G	H	I	J	K	L	M	N	O
8				W₄	E₁	A₁	R₁	Y₄							

| E₁ | F₄ | K₅ | O₁ | R₁ | S₁ | T₁ | 28 | ★ |

| A₁ | C₃ | F₄ | H₄ | I₁ | L₁ | Y₄ | 72 | ★★★ |

| A₁ | E₁ | E₁ | G₂ | H₄ | H₄ | L₁ | 30 | ★★ |

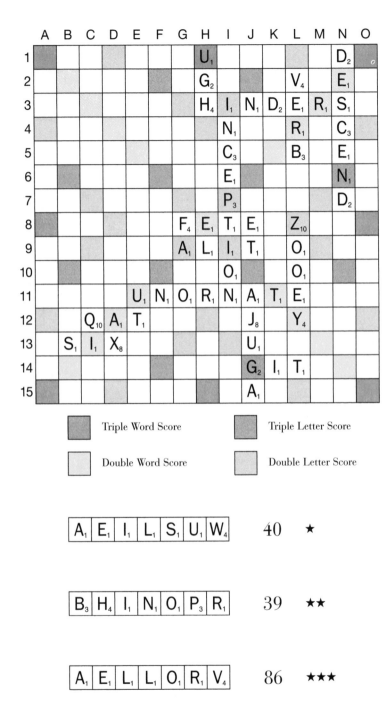

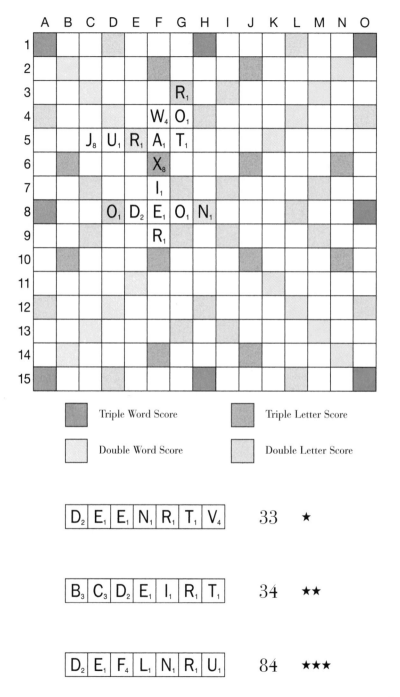

| | D₂ | E₁ | E₁ | N₁ | R₁ | T₁ | V₄ | | 33 | ★ |

| | B₃ | C₃ | D₂ | E₁ | I₁ | R₁ | T₁ | | 34 | ★★ |

| | D₂ | E₁ | F₄ | L₁ | N₁ | R₁ | U₁ | | 84 | ★★★ |

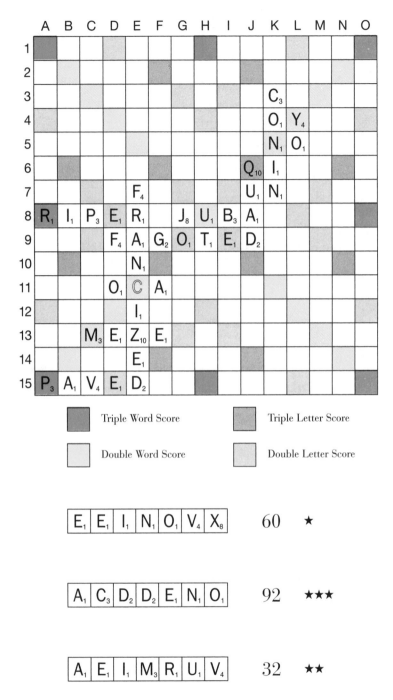

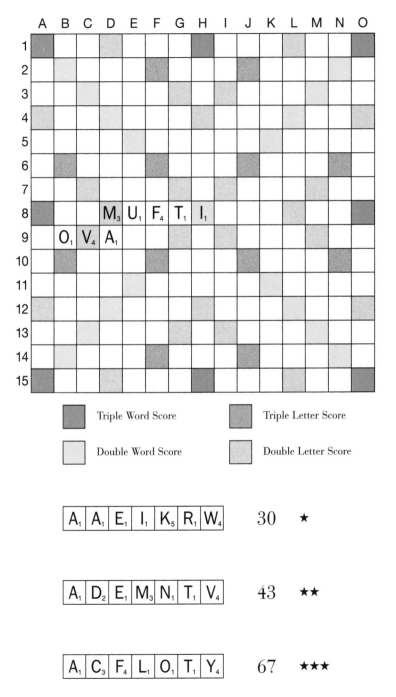

							M₃	U₁	F₄	T₁	I₁			
		O₁	V₄	A₁										

A₁	A₁	E₁	I₁	K₅	R₁	W₄		30	★
A₁	D₂	E₁	M₃	N₁	T₁	V₄		43	★★
A₁	C₃	F₄	L₁	O₁	T₁	Y₄		67	★★★

Triple Word Score   Triple Letter Score

Double Word Score   Double Letter Score

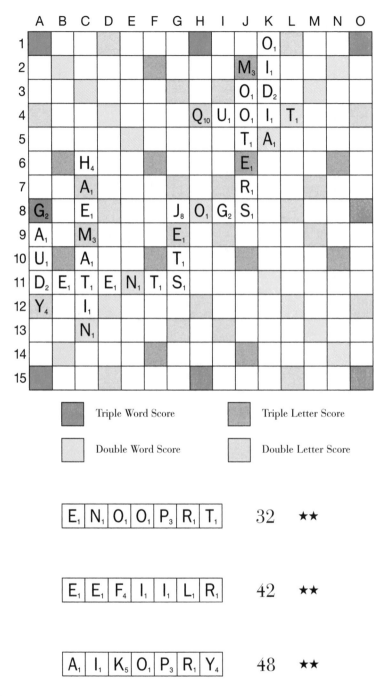

| | E₁ | N₁ | O₁ | O₁ | P₃ | R₁ | T₁ | | 32 | ★★ |

| | E₁ | E₁ | F₄ | I₁ | I₁ | L₁ | R₁ | | 42 | ★★ |

| | A₁ | I₁ | K₅ | O₁ | P₃ | R₁ | Y₄ | | 48 | ★★ |

	A	B	C	D	E	F	G	H	I	J	K	L	M	N	O
1															
2			B₃												
3			O₁												
4	J₈	U₁	R₁	A₁	T₁										
5			R₁												
6			O₁			D₂									
7		A₁	W₄		F₄	E₁	T₁								
8		V₄		W₄	O₁	M₃	A₁	N₁							
9		U₁			H₄	E₁	X₈								
10		L₁				A₁	I₁								
11		S₁				N₁									
12	A₁	I₁	K₅	I₁	D₂	O₁		C₃							
13		N₁				R₁		A₁							
14		G₂				S₁	O₁	R₁	D₂	I₁	N	I₁			
15							E₁			E₁	N₁	U₁	R₁	E₁

Triple Word Score   Triple Letter Score

Double Word Score   Double Letter Score

| A₁ | G₂ | I₁ | L₁ | N₁ | N₁ | V₄ | 36   ★★

| A₁ | E₁ | H₄ | I₁ | O₁ | R₁ | U₁ | 49   ★★

| A₁ | E₁ | F₄ | N₁ | O₁ | R₁ | Y₄ | 36   ★★

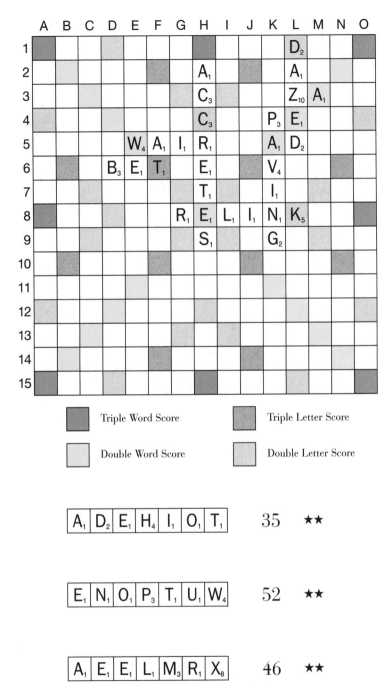

	A	B	C	D	E	F	G	H	I	J	K	L	M	N	O
1												D₂			
2								A₁				A₁			
3								C₃				Z₁₀	A₁		
4								C₃			P₃	E₁			
5					W₄	A₁	I₁	R₁			A₁	D₂			
6		B₃	E₁	T₁		E₁				V₄					
7								T₁			I₁				
8							R₁	E₁	L₁	I₁	N₁	K₅			
9								S₁			G₂				
10															
11															
12															
13															
14															
15															

Triple Word Score   Triple Letter Score

Double Word Score   Double Letter Score

A₁ D₂ E₁ H₄ I₁ O₁ T₁   35   ★★

E₁ N₁ O₁ P₃ T₁ U₁ W₄   52   ★★

A₁ E₁ E₁ L₁ M₃ R₁ X₈   46   ★★

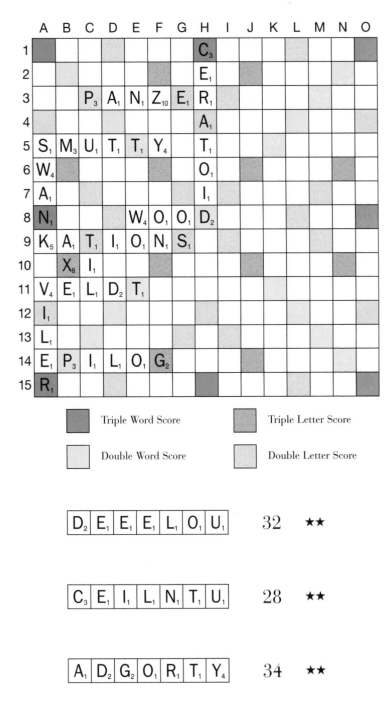

	A	B	C	D	E	F	G	H	I	J	K	L	M	N	O
1								C₃							
2								E₁							
3			P₃	A₁	N₁	Z₁₀	E₁	R₁							
4								A₁							
5	S₁	M₃	U₁	T₁	T₁	Y₄		T₁							
6	W₄							O₁							
7	A₁							I₁							
8	N₁				W₄	O₁	O₁	D₂							
9	K₅	A₁	T₁	I₁	O₁	N₁	S₁								
10		X₈	I₁												
11	V₄	E₁	L₁	D₂	T₁										
12	I₁														
13	L₁														
14	E₁	P₃	I₁	L₁	O₁	G₂									
15	R₁														

Triple Word Score   Triple Letter Score

Double Word Score   Double Letter Score

| D₂ | E₁ | E₁ | E₁ | L₁ | O₁ | U₁ | 32   ★★ |

| C₃ | E₁ | I₁ | L₁ | N₁ | T₁ | U₁ | 28   ★★ |

| A₁ | D₂ | G₂ | O₁ | R₁ | T₁ | Y₄ | 34   ★★ |

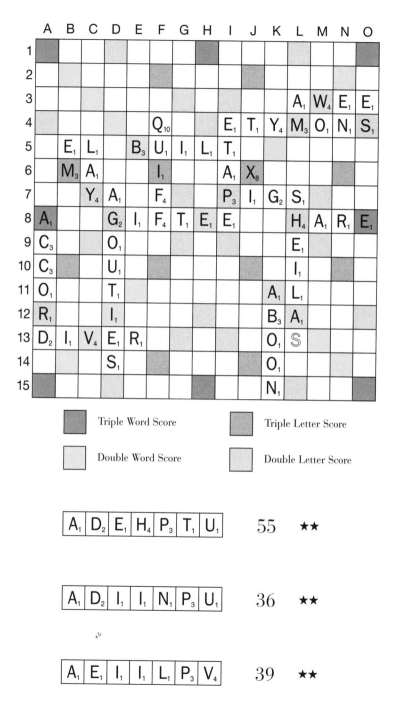

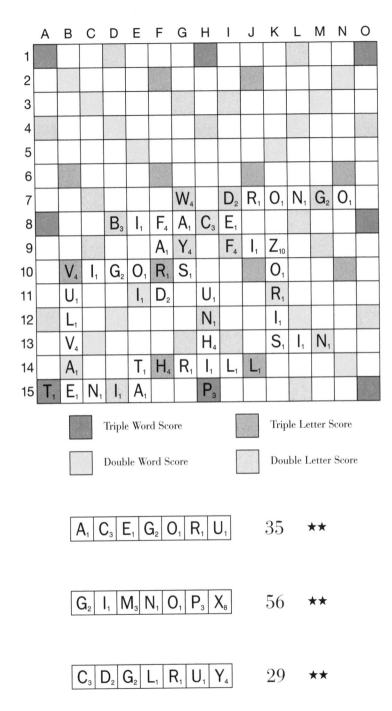

	A	B	C	D	E	F	G	H	I	J	K	L	M	N	O
1															
2															
3															
4															
5															
6															
7							W₄		D₂	R₁	O₁	N₁	G₂	O₁	
8				B₃	I₁	F₄	A₁	C₃	E₁						
9					A₁	Y₄		F₄	I₁	Z₁₀					
10	V₄	I₁	G₂	O₁	R₁	S₁				O₁					
11	U₁			I₁	D₂		U₁			R₁					
12	L₁						N₁			I₁					
13	V₄					H₄			S₁	I₁	N₁				
14	A₁		T₁	H₄	R₁	I₁	L₁	L₁							
15	T₁	E₁	N₁	I₁	A₁		P₃								

Triple Word Score   Triple Letter Score

Double Word Score   Double Letter Score

A₁ C₃ E₁ G₂ O₁ R₁ U₁   35   ★★

G₂ I₁ M₃ N₁ O₁ P₃ X₈   56   ★★

C₃ D₂ G₂ L₁ R₁ U₁ Y₄   29   ★★

E₁ G₂ H₄ I₁ P₃ R₁ U₁   45   ★★

A₁ H₄ I₁ L₁ O₁ U₁ Y₄   35   ★★

A₁ E₁ L₁ M₃ N₁ N₁ T₁   37   ★★

35 ☆

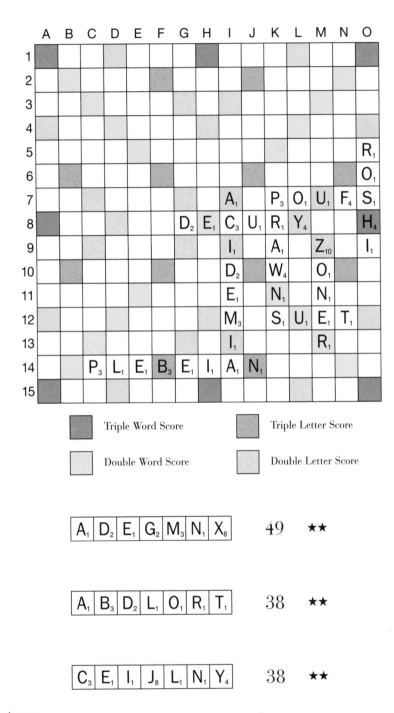

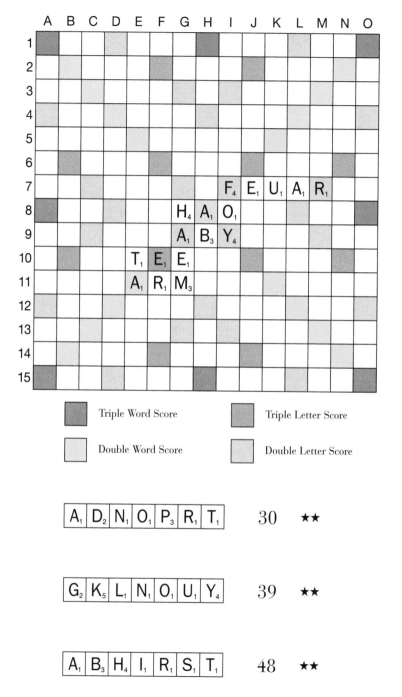

	A	B	C	D	E	F	G	H	I	J	K	L	M	N	O
7									F₄	E₁	U₁	A₁	R₁		
8							H₄	A₁	O₁						
9							A₁	B₃	Y₄						
10				T₁	E₁	E₁									
11				A₁	R₁	M₃									

Triple Word Score   Triple Letter Score

Double Word Score   Double Letter Score

A₁ D₂ N₁ O₁ P₃ R₁ T₁   30   ★★

G₂ K₅ L₁ N₁ O₁ U₁ Y₄   39   ★★

A₁ B₃ H₄ I₁ R₁ S₁ T₁   48   ★★

37 ☆

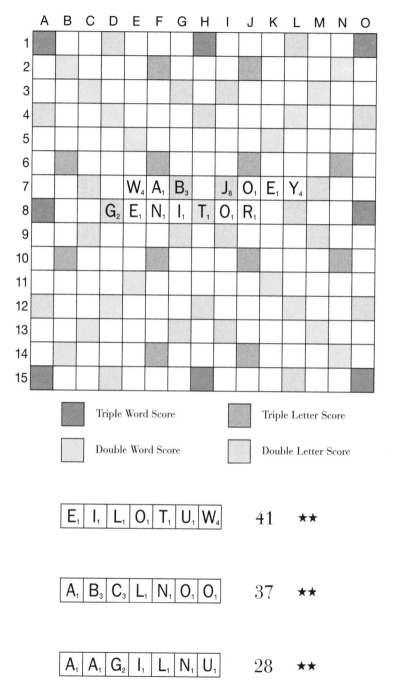

E_1	I_1	L_1	O_1	T_1	U_1	W_4

41 ★★

A_1	B_3	C_3	L_1	N_1	O_1	O_1

37 ★★

A_1	A_1	G_2	I_1	L_1	N_1	U_1

28 ★★

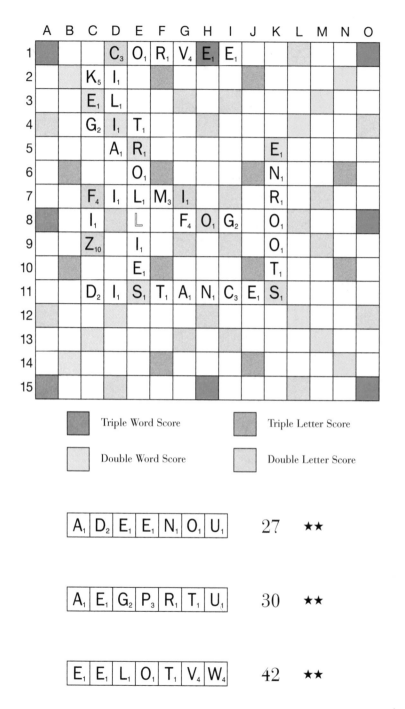

	A	B	C	D	E	F	G	H	I	J	K	L	M	N	O
1				C₃	O₁	R₁	V₄	E₁	E₁						
2			K₅	I₁											
3			E₁	L₁											
4			G₂	I₁	T₁										
5				A₁	R₁						E₁				
6					O₁						N₁				
7			F₄	I₁	L₁	M₃	I₁				R₁				
8			I₁		L		F₄	O₁	G₂		O₁				
9			Z₁₀		I₁						O₁				
10					E₁						T₁				
11			D₂	I₁	S₁	T₁	A₁	N₁	C₃	E₁	S₁				
12															
13															
14															
15															

Triple Word Score   Triple Letter Score

Double Word Score   Double Letter Score

A₁ D₂ E₁ E₁ N₁ O₁ U₁   27 ★★

A₁ E₁ G₂ P₃ R₁ T₁ U₁   30 ★★

E₁ E₁ L₁ O₁ T₁ V₄ W₄   42 ★★

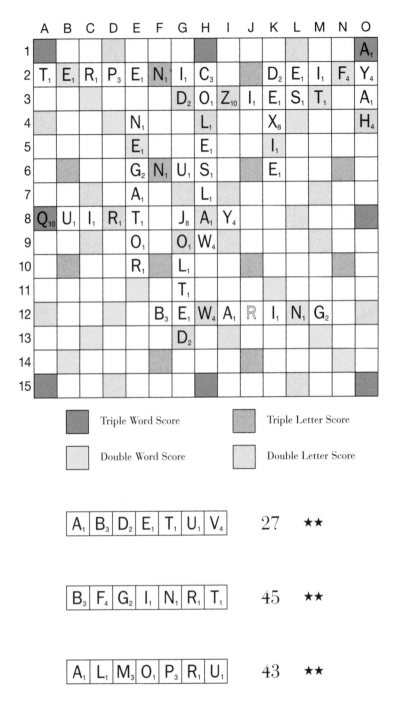

	A	B	C	D	E	F	G	H	I	J	K	L	M	N	O
1															A₁
2	T₁	E₁	R₁	P₃	E₁	N₁	I₁	C₃			D₂	E₁	I₁	F₄	Y₄
3							D₂	O₁	Z₁₀	I₁	E₁	S₁	T₁		A₁
4					N₁			L₁			X₈				H₄
5					E₁			E₁			I₁				
6					G₂	N₁	U₁	S₁			E₁				
7					A₁			L₁							
8	Q₁₀	U₁	I₁	R₁	T₁		J₈	A₁	Y₄						
9					O₁		O₁	W₄							
10					R₁		L₁								
11							T₁								
12						B₃	E₁	W₄	A₁	R	I₁	N₁	G₂		
13							D₂								
14															
15															

Triple Word Score   Triple Letter Score

Double Word Score   Double Letter Score

A₁ B₃ D₂ E₁ T₁ U₁ V₄   27   ★★

B₃ F₄ G₂ I₁ N₁ R₁ T₁   45   ★★

A₁ L₁ M₃ O₁ P₃ R₁ U₁   43   ★★

	A	B	C	D	E	F	G	H	I	J	K	L	M	N	O
1								T_1	U_1	X_8					
2								R_1							
3								A_1							
4								C_3	O_1	O_1	E_1	E_1			
5					T_1			H							
6					H_4			E_1							
7					E_1			A_1							
8		I_1	N_1	V_4	E_1	R_1	S_1	E_1							
9					L_1										
10					I_1	D_2									
11					N_1	O_1									
12						G_2									
13			H_4	A_1	Z_{10}	E_1									
14															
15															

Triple Word Score   Triple Letter Score

Double Word Score   Double Letter Score

| A_1 | C_3 | E_1 | G_2 | I_1 | L_1 | M_3 | | 35 | ★★ |

| D_2 | D_2 | E_1 | I_1 | O_1 | T_1 | Y_4 | | 39 | ★★ |

| A_1 | E_1 | E_1 | G_2 | I_1 | M_3 | O_1 | | 35 | ★★ |

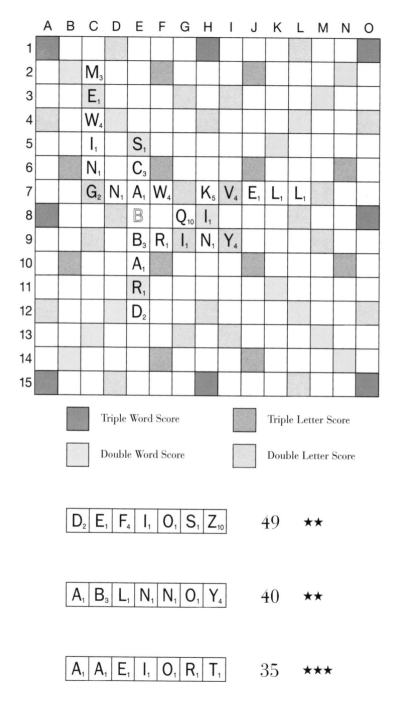

	A	B	C	D	E	F	G	H	I	J	K	L	M	N	O
1															
2			M₃												
3			E₁												
4			W₄												
5			I₁		S₁										
6			N₁		C₃										
7			G₂	N₁	A₁	W₄		K₅	V₄	E₁	L₁	L₁			
8					B		Q₁₀	I₁							
9					B₃	R₁	I₁	N₁	Y₄						
10					A₁										
11					R₁										
12					D₂										
13															
14															
15															

Triple Word Score   Triple Letter Score

Double Word Score   Double Letter Score

| D₂ | E₁ | F₄ | I₁ | O₁ | S₁ | Z₁₀ | 49   ★★

| A₁ | B₃ | L₁ | N₁ | N₁ | O₁ | Y₄ | 40   ★★

| A₁ | A₁ | E₁ | I₁ | O₁ | R₁ | T₁ | 35   ★★★

	A	B	C	D	E	F	G	H	I	J	K	L	M	N	O
1															E₁
2															X₈
3														F₄	E₁
4								O₁	C₃	T₁	O₁	P₃	O₁	D₂
5													R₁	
6						E₁	U₁	P₃	H₄	R₁	O₁	E₁	S₁
7					Q₁₀	I₁						R₁	
8					F₄	O₁	Y₄		T₁	H₄	R₁	A₁	W₄
9							A₁	V₄	A₁		N₁	
10				Z₁₀	I₁	G₂				K₅	
11															
12															
13															
14															
15															

Triple Word Score Triple Letter Score

Double Word Score Double Letter Score

C₃ D₂ G₂ N₁ O₁ T₁ U₁   33   ★★

A₁ G₂ L₁ O₁ O₁ T₁ U₁   25   ★★

C₃ G₂ I₁ L₁ R₁ T₁ V₄   24   ★★

	A	B	C	D	E	F	G	H	I	J	K	L	M	N	O
1															
2															
3															
4										L₁	O₁				
5										O₁	I₁				
6										U₁					
7										I₁					
8								H₄	O₁	N₁	E₁				
9								I₁							
10															
11															
12															
13															
14															
15															

Triple Word Score · Triple Letter Score

Double Word Score · Double Letter Score

A₁ E₁ I₁ N₁ N₁ R₁ Y₄ · 27 · ★

A₁ A₁ B₃ E₁ L₁ T₁ U₁ · 83 · ★★★

M₃ N₁ O₁ O₁ X₈ Y₄ Z₁₀ · 60 · ★★★

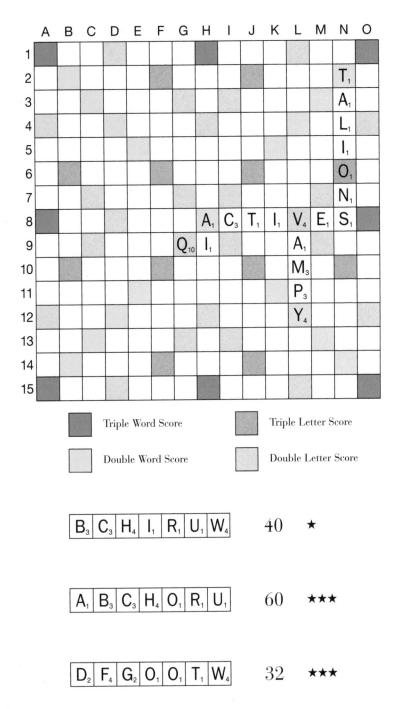

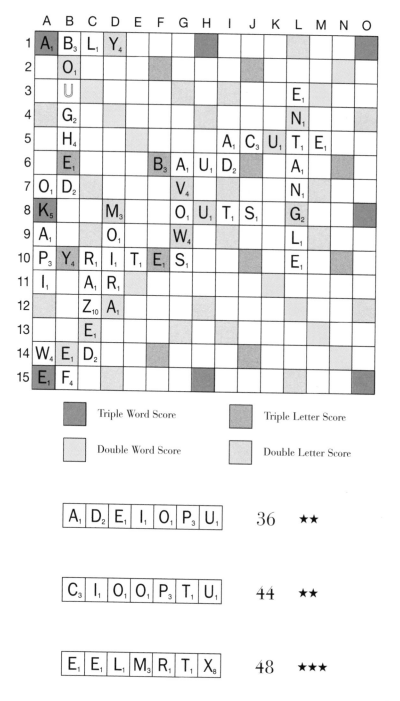

	A	B	C	D	E	F	G	H	I	J	K	L	M	N	O
1	A₁	B₃	L₁	Y₄											
2		O₁													
3		U										E₁			
4		G₂										N₁			
5		H₄						A₁	C₃	U₁	T₁	E₁			
6		E₁				B₃	A₁	U₁	D₂			A₁			
7	O₁	D₂					V₄					N₁			
8	K₅			M₃			O₁	U₁	T₁	S₁		G₂			
9	A₁			O₁			W₄					L₁			
10	P₃	Y₄	R₁	I₁	T₁	E₁	S₁					E₁			
11	I₁		A₁	R₁											
12			Z₁₀	A₁											
13			E₁												
14	W₄	E₁	D₂												
15	E₁	F₄													

- ■ Triple Word Score
- ■ Triple Letter Score
- ■ Double Word Score
- ■ Double Letter Score

A₁ D₂ E₁ I₁ O₁ P₃ U₁   36   ★★

C₃ I₁ O₁ O₁ P₃ T₁ U₁   44   ★★

E₁ E₁ L₁ M₃ R₁ T₁ X₈   48   ★★★

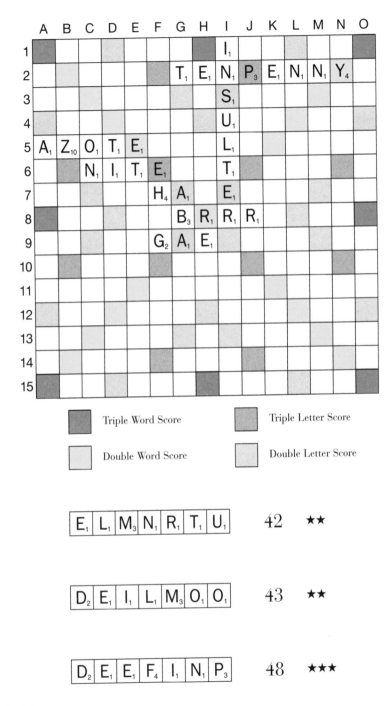

	A	B	C	D	E	F	G	H	I	J	K	L	M	N	O
1									I₁						
2							T₁	E₁	N₁	P₃	E₁	N₁	N₁	Y₄	
3									S₁						
4									U₁						
5	A₁	Z₁₀	O₁	T₁	E₁				L₁						
6			N₁	I₁	T₁	E₁			T₁						
7						H₄	A₁		E₁						
8							B₃	R₁	R₁	R₁					
9							G₂	A₁	E₁						
10															
11															
12															
13															
14															
15															

Triple Word Score   Triple Letter Score

Double Word Score   Double Letter Score

E₁ L₁ M₃ N₁ R₁ T₁ U₁   42   ★★

D₂ E₁ I₁ L₁ M₃ O₁ O₁   43   ★★

D₂ E₁ E₁ F₄ I₁ N₁ P₃   48   ★★★

☆ 50

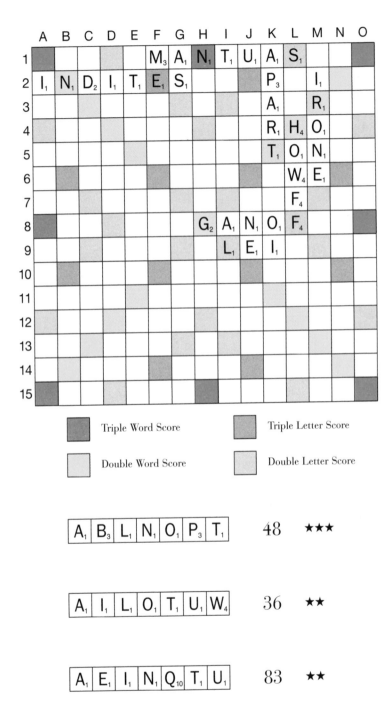

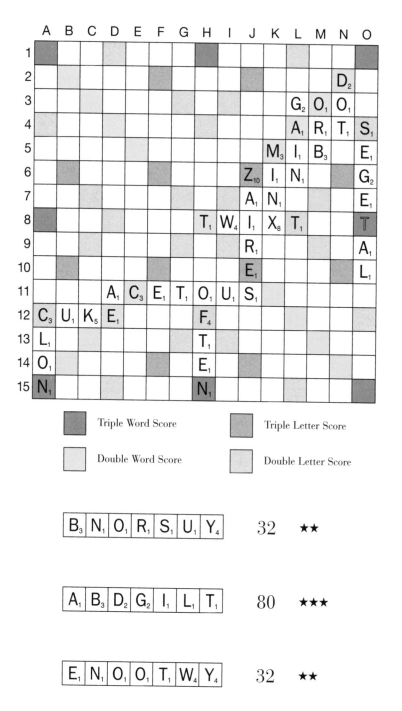

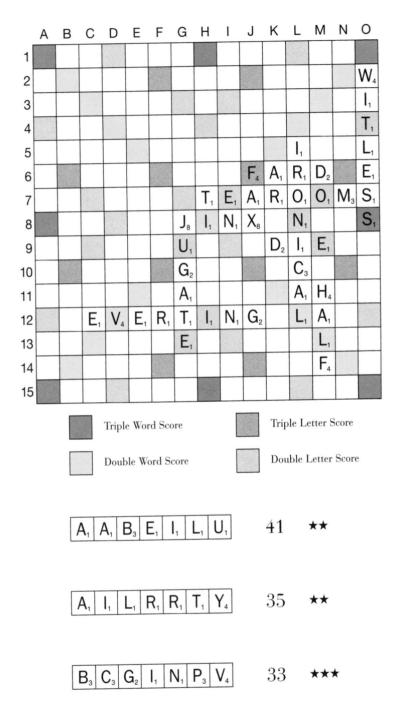

A₁ A₁ B₃ E₁ I₁ L₁ U₁   41   ★★

A₁ I₁ L₁ R₁ R₁ T₁ Y₄   35   ★★

B₃ C₃ G₂ I₁ N₁ P₃ V₄   33   ★★★

	A	B	C	D	E	F	G	H	I	J	K	L	M	N	O
1															
2										W₄					
3									C₃	H₄	A₁	I₁	R₁		
4									I₁						F₄
5										P₃	A₁	G₂	O₁	D₂	A₁
6							L₁	A₁	I₁	C₃					I₁
7					P₃		J₈		O₁						N₁
8				N₁	O₁	V₄	A₁		R₁						T₁
9				O₁		R₁			D₂						
10				F₄											
11															
12															
13															
14															
15															

Triple Word Score   Triple Letter Score

Double Word Score   Double Letter Score

A₁ I₁ I₁ N₁ O₁ S₁ V₄   76   ★★★

A₁ L₁ M₃ N₁ S₁ U₁ Y₄   41   ★★

D₂ E₁ G₂ I₁ R₁ U₁ W₄   32   ★★

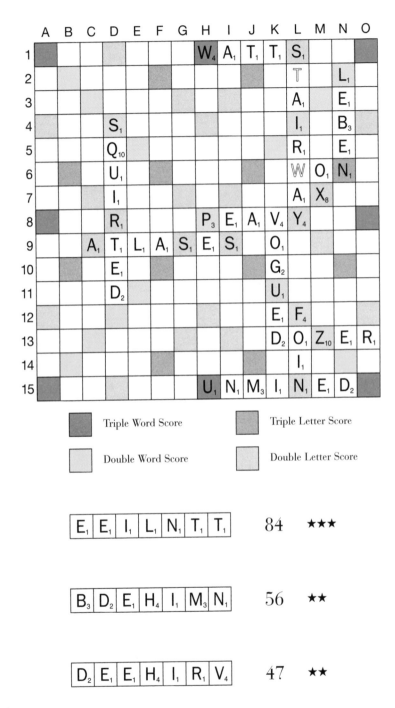

	A	B	C	D	E	F	G	H	I	J	K	L	M	N	O
1								W₄	A₁	T₁	T₁	S₁			
2												T		L₁	
3												A₁		E₁	
4				S₁								I₁		B₃	
5				Q₁₀								R₁		E₁	
6				U₁								W	O₁	N₁	
7				I₁								A₁	X₈		
8				R₁				P₃	E₁	A₁	V₄	Y₄			
9			A₁	T₁	L₁	A₁	S₁	E₁	S₁		O₁				
10				E₁							G₂				
11				D₂							U₁				
12											E₁	F₄			
13											D₂	O₁	Z₁₀	E₁	R₁
14												I₁			
15								U₁	N₁	M₃	I₁	N₁	E₁	D₂	

Triple Word Score   Triple Letter Score

Double Word Score   Double Letter Score

E₁ E₁ I₁ L₁ N₁ T₁ T₁   84   ★★★

B₃ D₂ E₁ H₄ I₁ M₃ N₁   56   ★★

D₂ E₁ E₁ H₄ I₁ R₁ V₄   47   ★★

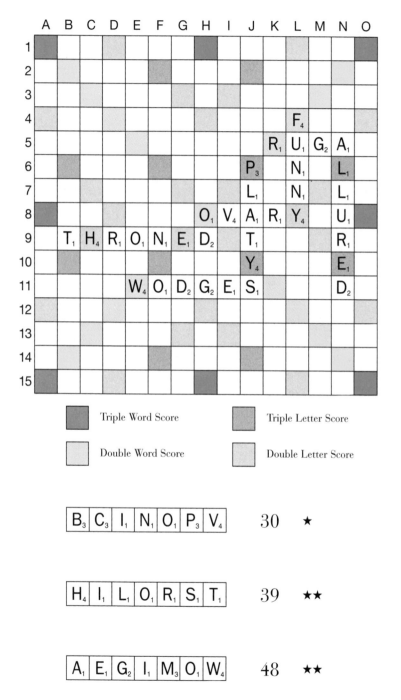

Triple Word Score

Triple Letter Score

Double Word Score

Double Letter Score

| B₃ | C₃ | I₁ | N₁ | O₁ | P₃ | V₄ | 30   ★

| H₄ | I₁ | L₁ | O₁ | R₁ | S₁ | T₁ | 39   ★★

| A₁ | E₁ | G₂ | I₁ | M₃ | O₁ | W₄ | 48   ★★

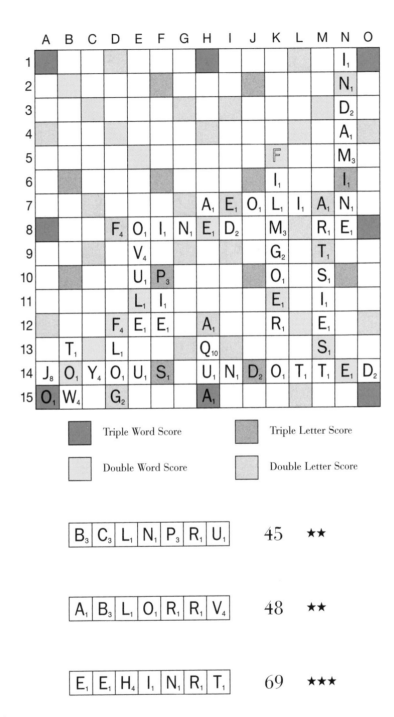

	A	B	C	D	E	F	G	H	I	J	K	L	M	N	O
1															
2															
3															
4															
5								A₁	E₁	R₁	O₁	B₃	A₁	T₁	
6						J₈	O₁	E₁							
7					E₁										
8					L₁	U₁	V₄								
9					L₁					L₁					
10					Y₄	O₁	G₂	E₁	E₁						
11								H₄							
12						F₄	I₁	O₁	R₁	D₂					
13			D₂	E₁	W₄	A₁	N₁								
14	A₁	N₁	N₁	E₁	X₈		R₁								
15							M₃								

Triple Word Score   Triple Letter Score

Double Word Score   Double Letter Score

A₁ F₄ I₁ L₁ O₁ O₁ R₁   41   ★★

G₂ G₂ I₁ N₁ N₁ O₁ R₁   74   ★★★

I₁ K₅ L₁ N₁ O₁ V₄ W₄   43   ★★

☆ 60

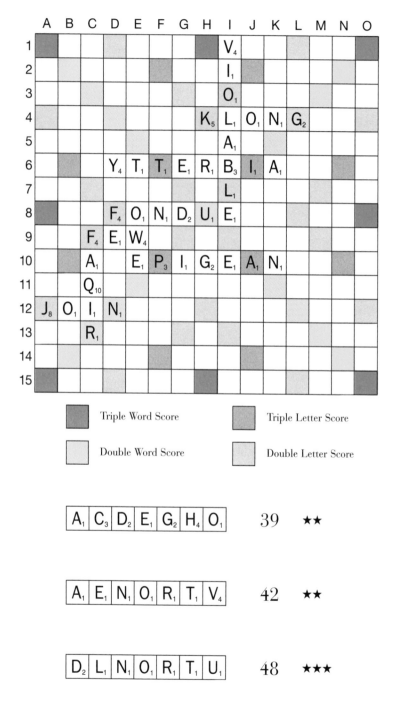

A₁ C₃ D₂ E₁ G₂ H₄ O₁   39   ★★

A₁ E₁ N₁ O₁ R₁ T₁ V₄   42   ★★

D₂ L₁ N₁ O₁ R₁ T₁ U₁   48   ★★★

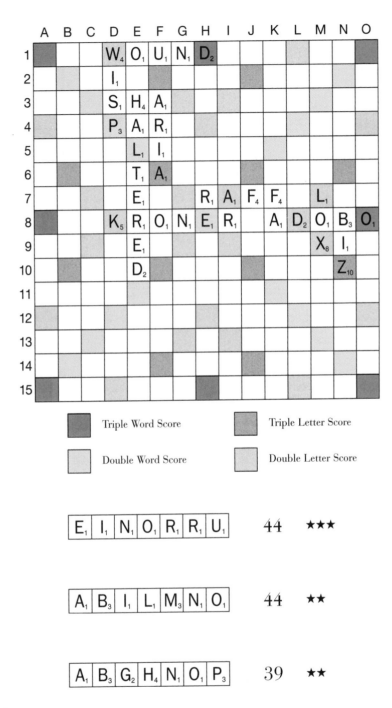

E₁ I₁ N₁ O₁ R₁ R₁ U₁   44   ★★★

A₁ B₃ I₁ L₁ M₃ N₁ O₁   44   ★★

A₁ B₃ G₂ H₄ N₁ O₁ P₃   39   ★★

| | A | A | F | I | L | O | T | | 38 | ★★ |

| | E | F | O | R | S | T | V | | 48 | ★★ |

| | A | B | I | L | M | O | P | | 36 | ★★★ |

| | B₃ | E₁ | H₄ | I₁ | P₃ | R₁ | Y₄ | | 38 | ★★ |

| | E₁ | H₄ | L₁ | O₁ | P₃ | S₁ | U₁ | | 48 | ★★ |

| | A₁ | A₁ | B₃ | G₂ | I₁ | L₁ | L₁ | | 34 | ★★★ |

	A	B	C	D	E	F	G	H	I	J	K	L	M	N	O
1															
2															
3															
4										R₁					
5										A₁	A₁				
6	J₈								X₈	I₁					
7	U₁							P₃		N₁					
8	M₃			Z₁₀		E₁	L₁	A₁	T₁	I₁	V₄	E₁	S₁		
9	P₃	E₁	N₁	I₁	C₃	I₁	L₁		V₄		E₁			I₁	
10		F₄	O₁	N₁				O₁		S₁			N₁		
11				C₃				N₁		T₁			U₁		
12				A₁			Q₁₀	I₁					A₁	Y₄	
13				T₁			U	N₁					T₁	A₁	
14				E₁			O₁	E₁					E₁	R₁	
15	B₃	O₁	G₂	S₁			D₂							E₁	

Triple Word Score   Triple Letter Score

Double Word Score   Double Letter Score

D₂ G₂ G₂ H₄ O₁ R₁ U₁   33   ★★

E₁ E₁ I₁ L₁ M₃ T₁ U₁   32   ★★

A₁ D₂ E₁ R₁ T₁ T₁ U₁   38   ★★★

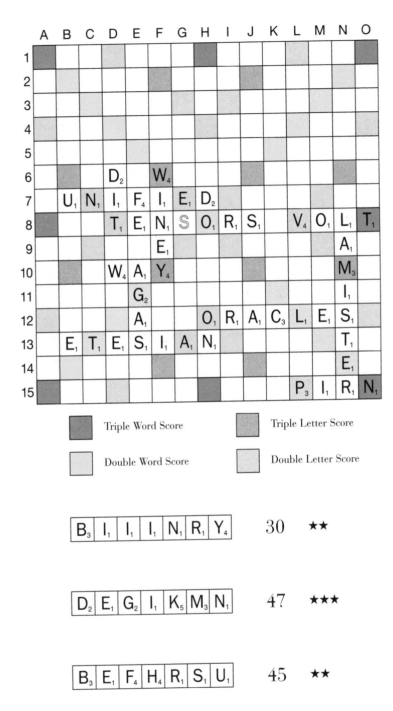

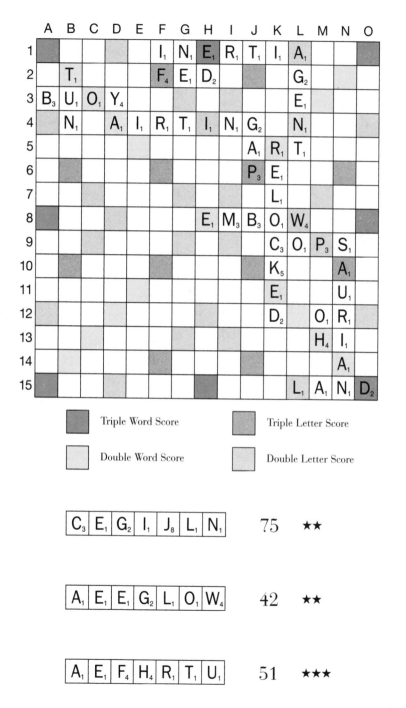

	A	B	C	D	E	F	G	H	I	J	K	L	M	N	O
1						I₁	N₁	E₁	R₁	T₁	I₁	A₁			
2		T₁				F₄	E₁	D₂				G₂			
3	B₃	U₁	O₁	Y₄								E₁			
4		N₁		A₁	I₁	R₁	T₁	I₁	N₁	G₂		N₁			
5									A₁	R₁	T₁				
6								P₃	E₁						
7									L₁						
8						E₁	M₃	B₃	O₁	W₄					
9								C₃	O₁	P₃	S₁				
10								K₅			A₁				
11								E₁			U₁				
12								D₂		O₁	R₁				
13										H₄	I₁				
14											A₁				
15										L₁	A₁	N₁	D₂		

Triple Word Score   Triple Letter Score

Double Word Score   Double Letter Score

C₃ E₁ G₂ I₁ J₈ L₁ N₁   75   ★★

A₁ E₁ E₁ G₂ L₁ O₁ W₄   42   ★★

A₁ E₁ F₄ H₄ R₁ T₁ U₁   51   ★★★

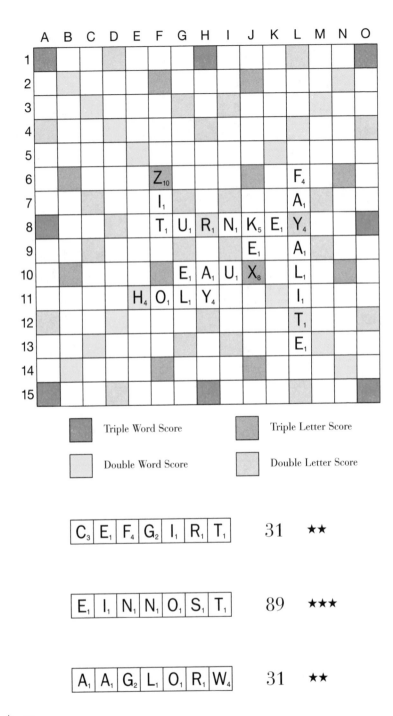

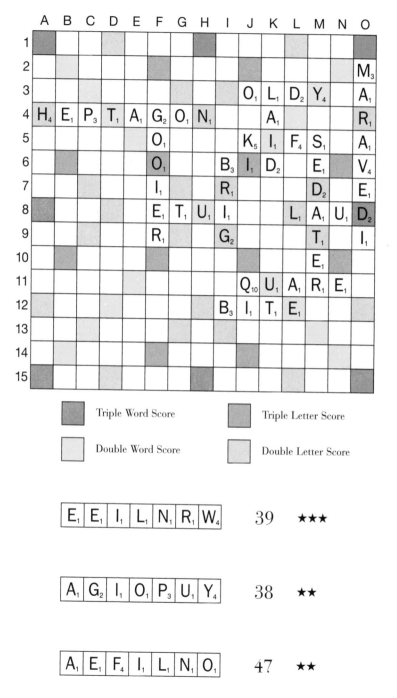

| | E₁ | E₁ | I₁ | L₁ | N₁ | R₁ | W₄ | | 39 | ★★★ |

| | A₁ | G₂ | I₁ | O₁ | P₃ | U₁ | Y₄ | | 38 | ★★ |

| | A₁ | E₁ | F₄ | I₁ | L₁ | N₁ | O₁ | | 47 | ★★ |

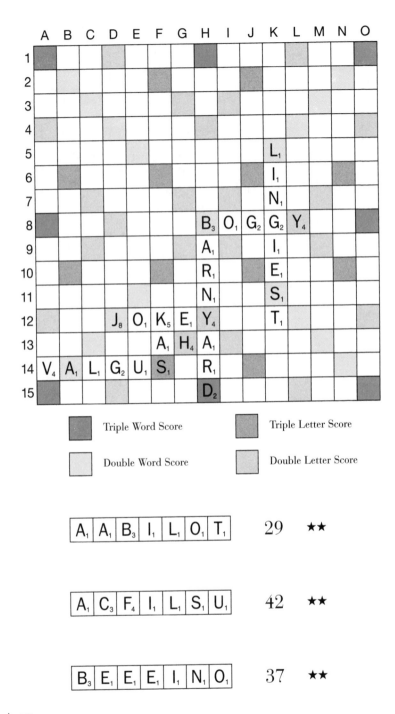

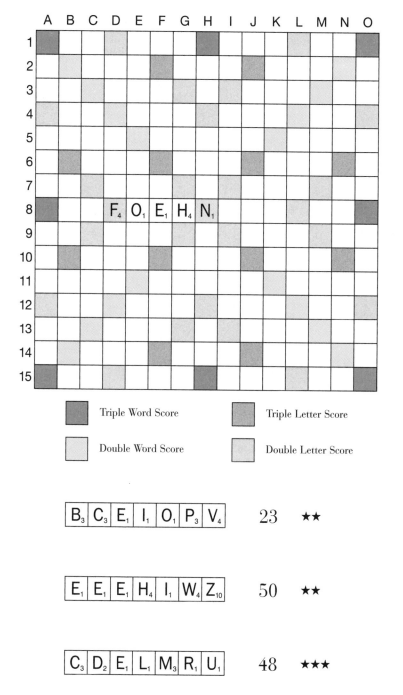

A₁ B₃ M₃ N₁ O₁ O₁ P₃   30   ★★

E₁ G₂ H₄ I₁ P₃ R₁ S₁   45   ★★

A₁ C₃ H₄ I₁ N₁ N₁ T₁   57   ★★★

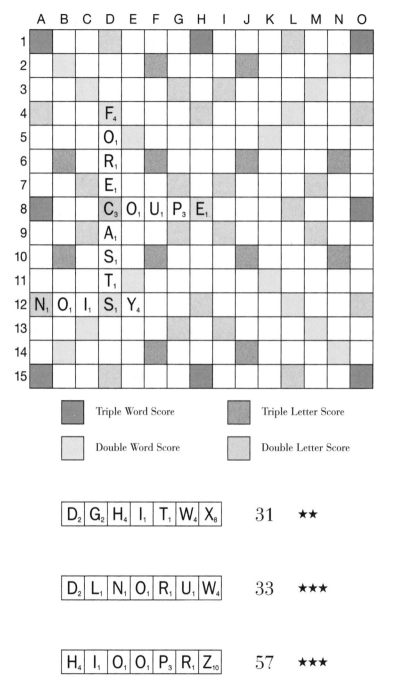

	A	B	C	D	E	F	G	H	I	J	K	L	M	N	O
1															
2															
3															
4				F$_4$											
5				O$_1$											
6				R$_1$											
7				E$_1$											
8				C$_3$	O$_1$	U$_1$	P$_3$	E$_1$							
9				A$_1$											
10				S$_1$											
11				T$_1$											
12	N$_1$	O$_1$	I$_1$	S$_1$	Y$_4$										
13															
14															
15															

Triple Word Score   Triple Letter Score

Double Word Score   Double Letter Score

| D$_2$ | G$_2$ | H$_4$ | I$_1$ | T$_1$ | W$_4$ | X$_8$ | 31 ★★

| D$_2$ | L$_1$ | N$_1$ | O$_1$ | R$_1$ | U$_1$ | W$_4$ | 33 ★★★

| H$_4$ | I$_1$ | O$_1$ | O$_1$ | P$_3$ | R$_1$ | Z$_{10}$ | 57 ★★★

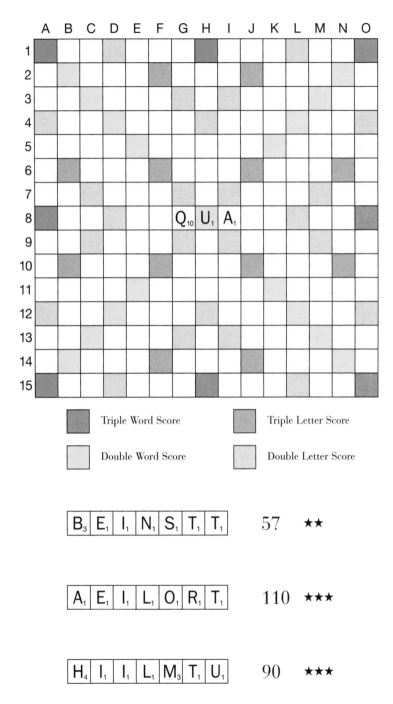

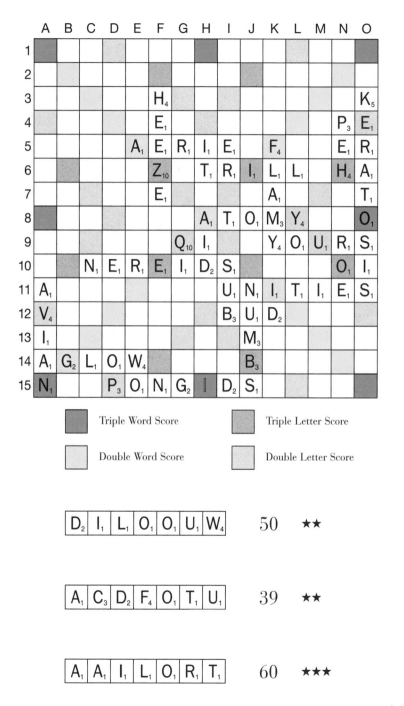

	A	B	C	D	E	F	G	H	I	J	K	L	M	N	O
1															
2															
3					H₄									K₅
4					E₁								P₃	E₁
5				A₁	E₁	R₁	I₁	E₁		F₄			E₁	R₁
6					Z₁₀		T₁	R₁	I₁	L₁	L₁		H₄	A₁
7					E₁				A₁				T₁
8							A₁	T₁	O₁	M₃	Y₄		O₁
9						Q₁₀	I₁		Y₄	O₁	U₁	R₁	S₁
10		N₁	E₁	R₁	E₁	I₁	D₂	S₁				O₁	I₁
11	A₁							U₁	N₁	I₁	T₁	I₁	E₁	S₁
12	V₄						B₃	U₁	D₂			
13	I₁							M₃			
14	A₁	G₂	L₁	O₁	W₄			B₃			
15	N₁		P₃	O₁	N₁	G₂	I	D₂	S₁			

Triple Word Score   Triple Letter Score

Double Word Score   Double Letter Score

D₂ I₁ L₁ O₁ O₁ U₁ W₄   50   ★★

A₁ C₃ D₂ F₄ O₁ T₁ U₁   39   ★★

A₁ A₁ I₁ L₁ O₁ R₁ T₁   60   ★★★

79 ☆

	A	B	C	D	E	F	G	H	I	J	K	L	M	N	O
1								Y$_4$		W$_4$	O$_1$	E$_1$	F$_4$	U$_1$	L$_1$
2								O$_1$	S$_1$	E$_1$			E$_1$	T$_1$	
3								N$_1$	A$_1$	E$_1$		U$_1$	H$_4$		
4								I$_1$	T$_1$		O$_1$				
5									I$_1$		C$_3$				
6								R$_1$	A$_1$	J$_8$	A$_1$				
7									B$_3$						
8	O$_1$	V$_4$	E$_1$	R$_1$				G$_2$	L$_1$	O$_1$	A$_1$	M$_3$			
9		I$_1$						O$_1$	E$_1$		M$_3$	I$_1$	X$_8$	T$_1$	
10		R$_1$						R$_1$							
11		U$_1$		P$_3$	A$_1$	G$_2$	O$_1$	D$_2$	A$_1$						
12		C$_3$						I$_1$							
13	W$_4$	I$_1$	Z$_{10}$	E$_1$	N$_1$			T$_1$							
14		D$_2$						A$_1$							
15	S$_1$	E$_1$	A$_1$	L$_1$	I$_1$	F$_4$	T$_1$	S$_1$							

Triple Word Score Triple Letter Score

Double Word Score Double Letter Score

| A$_1$ | D$_2$ | E$_1$ | I$_1$ | N$_1$ | O$_1$ | U$_1$ | 34 | ★★ |

| D$_2$ | H$_4$ | I$_1$ | L$_1$ | T$_1$ | U$_1$ | Y$_4$ | 49 | ★★★ |

| A$_1$ | I$_1$ | N$_1$ | O$_1$ | S$_1$ | T$_1$ | V$_4$ | 33 | ★★ |

☆ 80

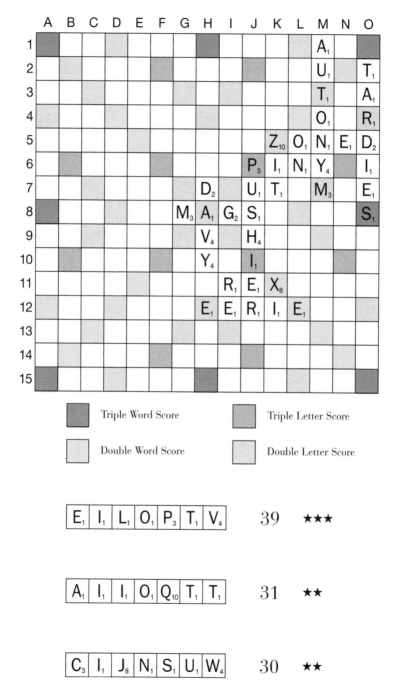

| | E₁ | I₁ | L₁ | O₁ | P₃ | T₁ | V₄ | | 39 | ★★★ |

| | A₁ | I₁ | I₁ | O₁ | Q₁₀ | T₁ | T₁ | | 31 | ★★ |

| | C₃ | I₁ | J₈ | N₁ | S₁ | U₁ | W₄ | | 30 | ★★ |

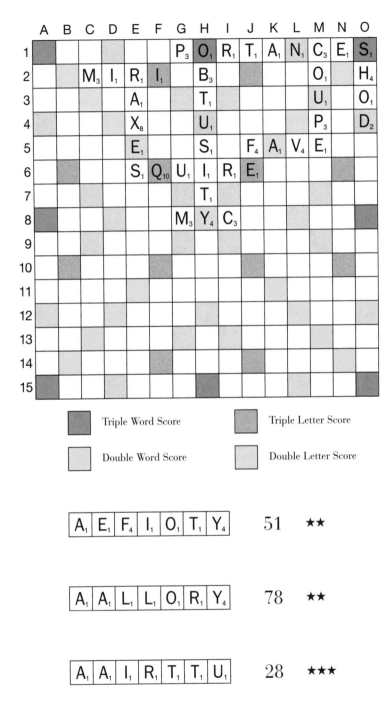

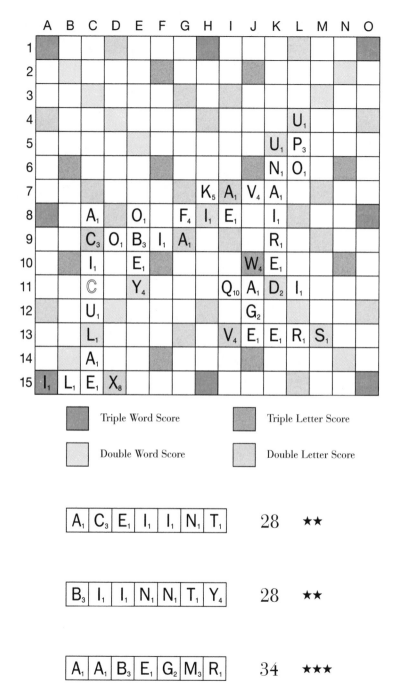

											U₁			
									U₁	P₃				
									N₁	O₁				
						K₅	A₁	V₄	A₁					
	A₁		O₁		F₄	I₁	E₁		I₁					
	C₃	O₁	B₃	I₁	A₁				R₁					
	I₁		E₁					W₄	E₁					
	C		Y₄				Q₁₀	A₁	D₂	I₁				
	U₁							G₂						
	L₁						V₄	E₁	E₁	R₁	S₁			
	A₁													
I₁	L₁	E₁	X₈											

| A₁ | C₃ | E₁ | I₁ | I₁ | N₁ | T₁ | | 28 | ★★ |

| B₃ | I₁ | I₁ | N₁ | N₁ | T₁ | Y₄ | | 28 | ★★ |

| A₁ | A₁ | B₃ | E₁ | G₂ | M₃ | R₁ | | 34 | ★★★ |

	A	B	C	D	E	F	G	H	I	J	K	L	M	N	O
1	B₃			L₁								C₃			O₁
2	U₁	P₃	G₂	I₁	R₁	D₂					M₃	A₁	J₈	O₁	R₁
3	N₁			T₁								L₁			A₁
4	K₅			A₁			Q₁₀					T₁			
5				N₁		O₁	U₁	T₁	W₄	O₁	R₁	E₁			
6				I₁			A₁					O₁			
7	V₄	I₁	X₈	E₁	N₁	A₁	L₁				P				
8			S₁	O₁	N₁	N₁	I₁	E₁	S₁		S₁	H₄	A₁	Y₄	
9					I₁	F₄					A₁				
10					Y₄						S₁				
11											T₁				
12											I₁				
13											E₁				
14											R₁				
15															

Triple Word Score   Triple Letter Score

Double Word Score   Double Letter Score

| E₁ | I₁ | L₁ | O₁ | R₁ | T₁ | U₁ | 62   ★★★★

| A₁ | E₁ | H₄ | R₁ | T₁ | T₁ | U₁ | 57   ★★

| A₁ | B₃ | E₁ | H₄ | O₁ | P₃ | U₁ | 43   ★★

											P₃	E₁	A₁	G₂
													E₁	
													R₁	
													I₁	
			P₃	O₁	L₁	I₁	C₃	Y₄					E₁	
							W₄	A₁	I₁	V₄	E₁	D₂	
		B₃			Q₁₀		M₃							
F₄	O₁	X₈	T₁	A₁	I₁	L₁	S₁						
E₁	T₁	U₁	I₁			A₁							
Z₁₀						U₁							
						G₂							
						H₄							
						E₁							
						R₁							
						S₁							

Triple Word Score   Triple Letter Score

Double Word Score   Double Letter Score

A₁ G₂ L₁ L₁ N₁ O₁ R₁   24   ★★

D₂ E₁ I₁ S₁ T₁ U₁ W₄   48   ★★★

E₁ I₁ J₈ L₁ R₁ W₄ Y₄   64   ★★★

85 ☆

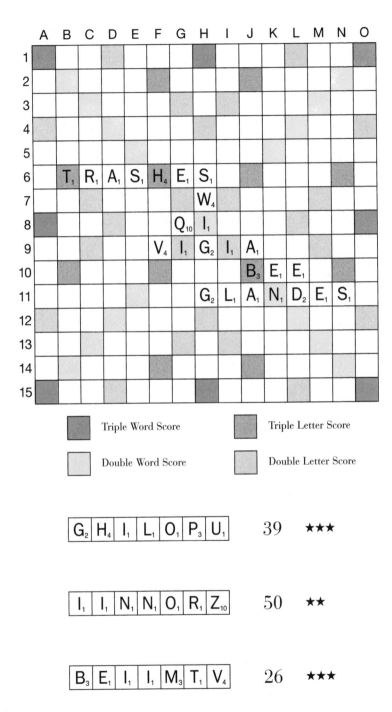

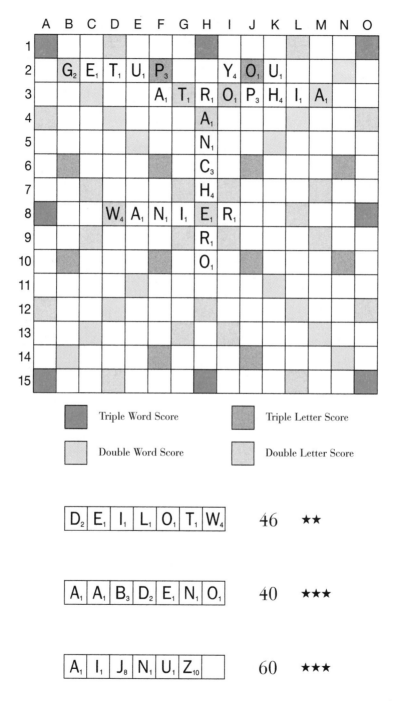

Triple Word Score

Triple Letter Score

Double Word Score

Double Letter Score

| D₂ | E₁ | I₁ | L₁ | O₁ | T₁ | W₄ | 46 ★★ |

| A₁ | A₁ | B₃ | D₂ | E₁ | N₁ | O₁ | 40 ★★★ |

| A₁ | I₁ | J₈ | N₁ | U₁ | Z₁₀ | 60 ★★★ |

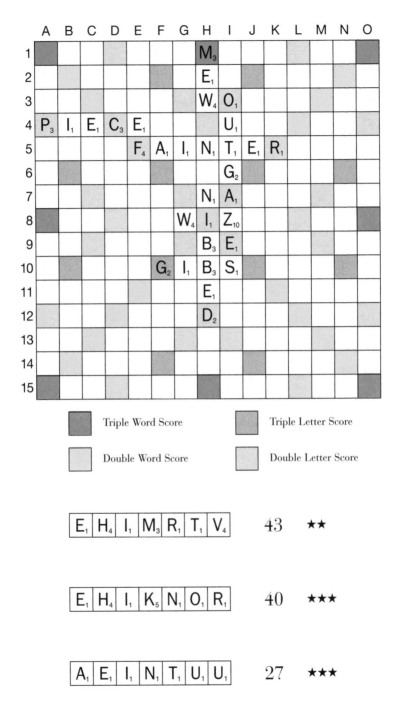

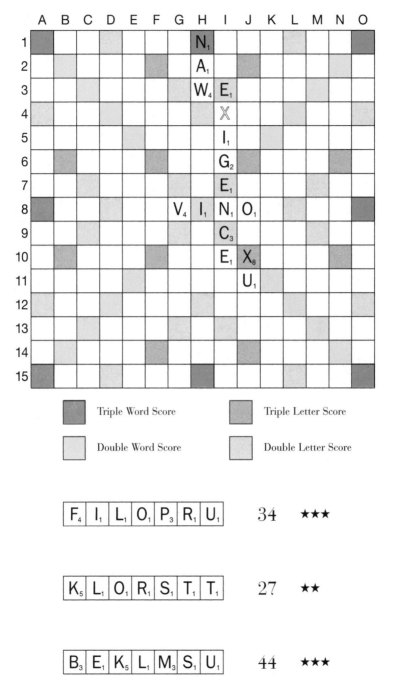

| | F₄ | I₁ | L₁ | O₁ | P₃ | R₁ | U₁ | | 34 | ★★★ |

| | K₅ | L₁ | O₁ | R₁ | S₁ | T₁ | T₁ | | 27 | ★★ |

| | B₃ | E₁ | K₅ | L₁ | M₃ | S₁ | U₁ | | 44 | ★★★ |

	A	B	C	D	E	F	G	H	I	J	K	L	M	N	O
1															B₃
2														F₄	A₁
3														O₁	
4										M₃	A₁	G₂	E₁		
5									A₁	V₄	O₁	W₄			
6										U₁		L₁	I₁	N₁	T₁
7										G₂					O₁
8						J₈	A₁	Y₄	S₁						W₄
9					P₃	O₁	N₁	E₁							E₁
10							A₁	T₁	A₁	X₈	I₁	A₁			L₁
11									N₁	I₁	D₂	I₁			
12															
13															
14															
15															

Triple Word Score   Triple Letter Score

Double Word Score   Double Letter Score

C₃ I₁ L₁ O₁ P₃ T₁ Y₄   51   ★★★

A₁ D₂ D₂ I₁ N₁ O₁ R₁   74   ★★★

E₁ F₄ G₂ H₄ L₁ M₃ P₃   36   ★★

☆ 90

	A	B	C	D	E	F	G	H	I	J	K	L	M	N	O
1															
2															
3															
4										C₃					
5										E₁	F₄				
6										P₃	E₁				
7										D₂					
8							J₈	I₁	N₁	K₅	S₁				
9										E₁					
10				U₁		G₂	L₁	U₁	E₁	Y₄					
11				L₁				M₃							
12				V₄				P₃	U₁	N₁	T₁	O₁			
13			W₄	A₁	R₁	I₁	E₁	S₁	T₁						
14															
15															

Triple Word Score   Triple Letter Score

Double Word Score   Double Letter Score

A₁ A₁ A₁ C₃ L₁ M₃ N₁   79   ★★★

C₃ E₁ H₄ L₁ S₁ T₁ Y₄   45   ★★

D₂ E₁ E₁ I₁ I₁ M₃   80   ★★★

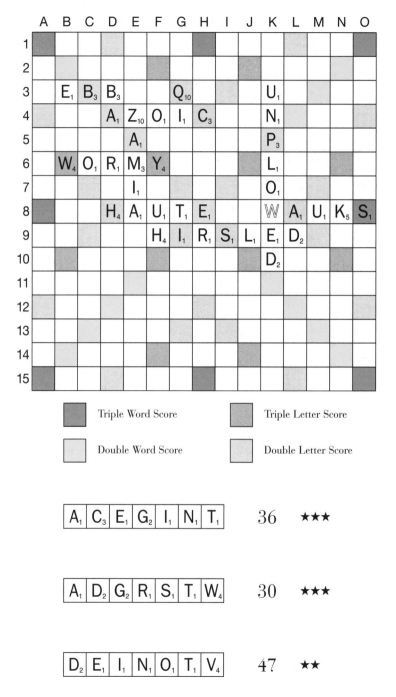

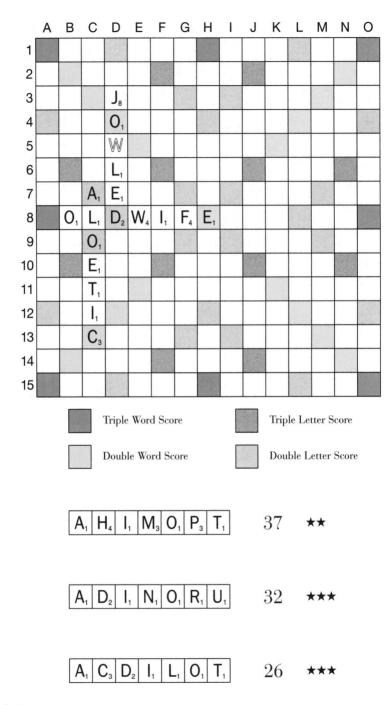

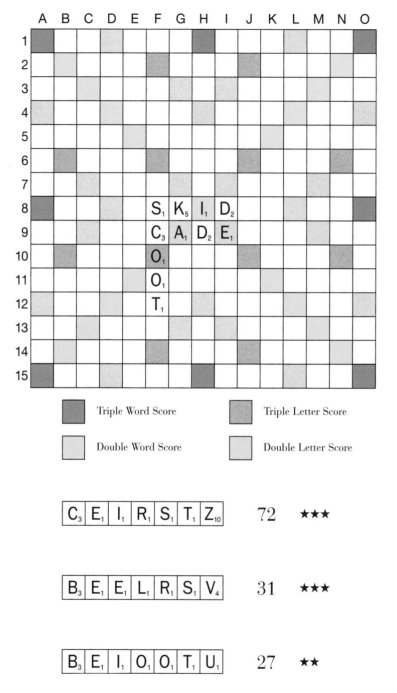

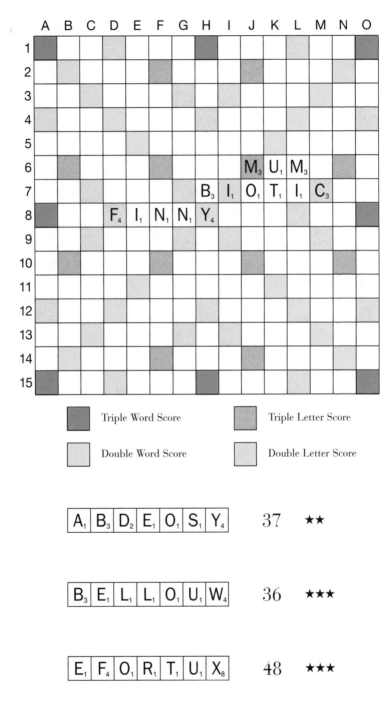

Triple Word Score   Triple Letter Score

Double Word Score   Double Letter Score

A₁ C₃ I₁ I₁ N₁ O₁ O₁   19   ★★

E₁ K₅ M₃ O₁ O₁ R₁ W₄   54   ★★★

A₁ E₁ E₁ F₄ L₁ R₁ W₄   80   ★★★

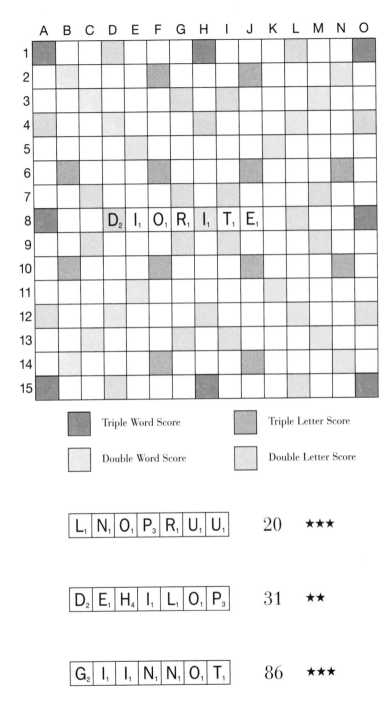

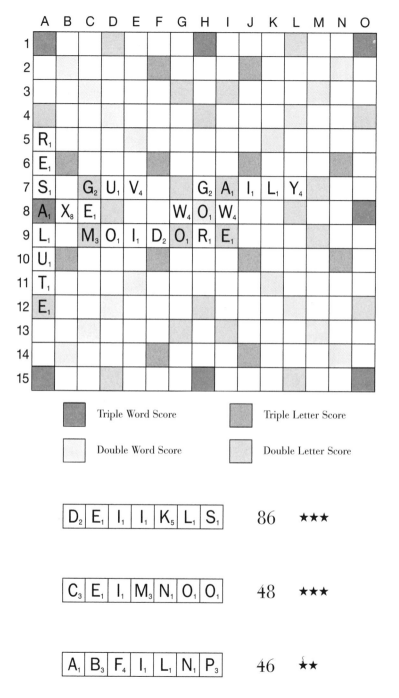

	A	B	C	D	E	F	G	H	I	J	K	L	M	N	O
1															
2															
3															
4															
5	R₁														
6	E₁														
7	S₁		G₂	U₁	V₄			G₂	A₁	I₁	L₁	Y₄			
8	A₁	X₈	E₁				W₄	O₁	W₄						
9	L₁		M₃	O₁	I₁	D₂	O₁	R₁	E₁						
10	U₁														
11	T₁														
12	E₁														
13															
14															
15															

Triple Word Score   Triple Letter Score

Double Word Score   Double Letter Score

D₂ E₁ I₁ I₁ K₅ L₁ S₁   86   ★★★

C₃ E₁ I₁ M₃ N₁ O₁ O₁   48   ★★★

A₁ B₃ F₄ I₁ L₁ N₁ P₃   46   ★★

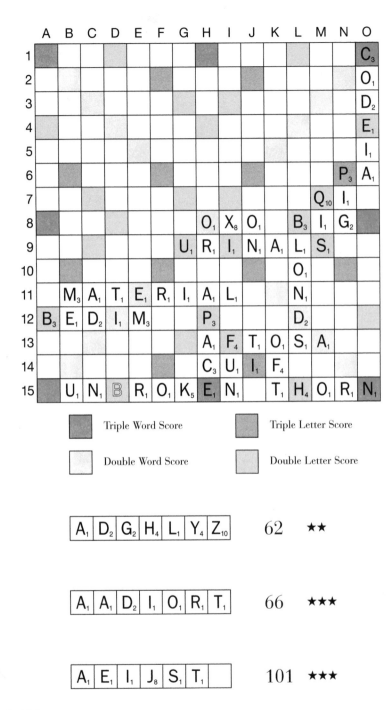

☆ 100

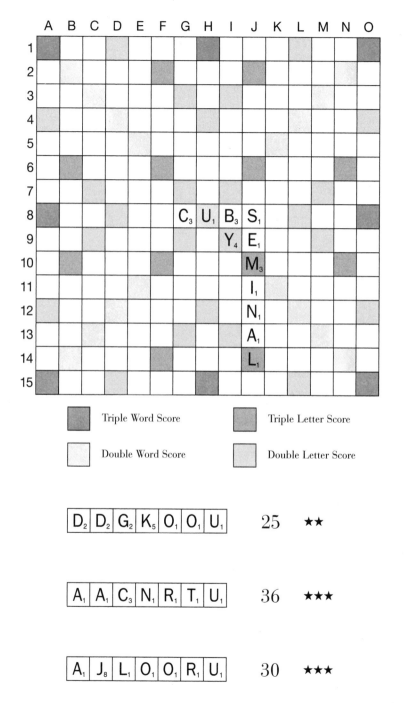

	A	B	C	D	E	F	G	H	I	J	K	L	M	N	O
8							C₃	U₁	B₃	S₁					
9									Y₄	E₁					
10										M₃					
11										I₁					
12										N₁					
13										A₁					
14										L₁					

Triple Word Score   Triple Letter Score

Double Word Score   Double Letter Score

D₂ D₂ G₂ K₅ O₁ O₁ U₁   25   ★★

A₁ A₁ C₃ N₁ R₁ T₁ U₁   36   ★★★

A₁ J₈ L₁ O₁ O₁ R₁ U₁   30   ★★★

101 ☆

	A	B	C	D	E	F	G	H	I	J	K	L	M	N	O
1	H₄														
2	O₁														
3	O₁	R₁													
4	T₁	I₁													
5		P₃													
6		A₁													
7		R₁		D₂					T₁						
8	L₁	I₁	Q₁₀	U₁	O₁	R₁		B₃	U₁	N₁	N₁	Y₄			
9		A₁		M₃					F₄						
10	E₁	N₁		P₃					T₁						
11	X₈		B₃	E₁	E₁	F	I₁	L₁	Y₄						
12	C₃			R₁											
13	I₁														
14	S₁														
15	E₁														

Triple Word Score   Triple Letter Score

Double Word Score   Double Letter Score

F₄ I₁ O₁ O₁ R₁ T₁ U₁   24   ★★

D₂ E₁ F₄ I₁ O₁ R₁ U₁   44   ★★★

A₁ D₂ H₄ M₃ N₁ O₁ U₁   38   ★★★

☆ 102

	A	B	C	D	E	F	G	H	I	J	K	L	M	N	O
1								W$_4$							
2								I$_1$							
3								N$_1$							
4								O$_1$	R$_1$						
5									U$_1$						
6				O$_1$				O$_1$	N$_1$						
7				U$_1$				O$_1$	N$_1$						
8				T$_1$		F$_4$		R$_1$	Y$_4$						
9				D$_2$			O$_1$	I$_1$							
10				O$_1$			R$_1$	E$_1$							
11				I$_1$			T$_1$								
12				N$_1$	U$_1$	D$_2$	E$_1$								
13				G$_2$			S$_1$	T$_1$	A$_1$	D$_2$	I$_1$	A$_1$	S$_1$		
14															
15															

Triple Word Score   Triple Letter Score

Double Word Score   Double Letter Score

A$_1$ C$_3$ E$_1$ H$_4$ M$_3$ N$_1$ N$_1$ 114 ★★★★

A$_1$ D$_2$ E$_1$ I$_1$ K$_5$ M$_3$ S$_1$ 49 ★★

C$_3$ H$_4$ I$_1$ N$_1$ P$_3$ S$_1$ X$_8$ 71 ★★

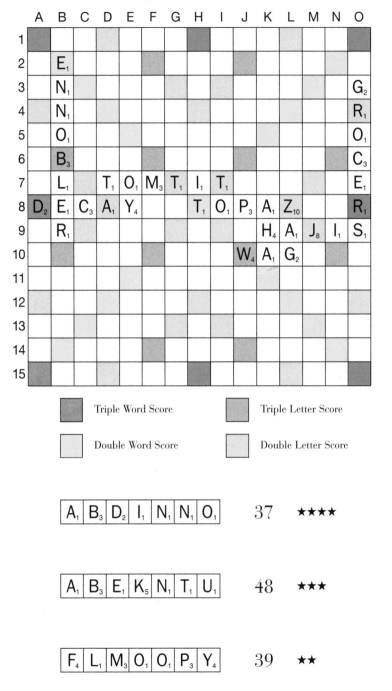

	A	B	C	D	E	F	G	H	I	J	K	L	M	N	O
1															
2		E₁													
3		N₁													G₂
4		N₁													R₁
5		O₁													O₁
6		B₃													C₃
7		L₁		T₁	O₁	M₃	T₁	I₁	T₁						E₁
8	D₂	E₁	C₃	A₁	Y₄			T₁	O₁	P₃	A₁	Z₁₀			R₁
9		R₁									H₄	A₁	J₈	I₁	S₁
10										W₄	A₁	G₂			
11															
12															
13															
14															
15															

Triple Word Score   Triple Letter Score

Double Word Score   Double Letter Score

A₁ B₃ D₂ I₁ N₁ N₁ O₁   37   ★★★★

A₁ B₃ E₁ K₅ N₁ T₁ U₁   48   ★★★

F₄ L₁ M₃ O₁ O₁ P₃ Y₄   39   ★★

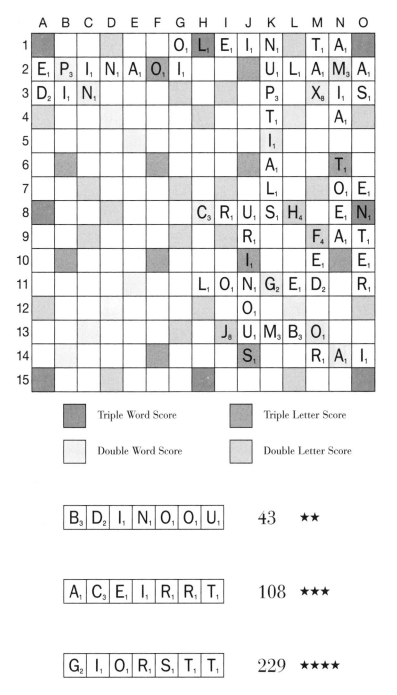

	A	B	C	D	E	F	G	H	I	J	K	L	M	N	O
1								O₁	L₁	E₁	I₁	N₁		T₁	A₁	
2	E₁	P₃	I₁	N₁	A₁	O₁	I₁				U₁	L₁	A₁	M₃	A₁
3	D₂	I₁	N₁								P₃		X₈	I₁	S₁
4											T₁			A₁	
5											I₁				
6											A₁			T₁	
7											L₁			O₁	E₁
8								C₃	R₁	U₁	S₁	H₄		E₁	N₁
9									R₁				F₄	A₁	T₁
10										I₁			E₁		E₁
11							L₁	O₁	N₁	G₂	E₁	D₂			R₁
12										O₁					
13										J₈	U₁	M₃	B₃	O₁	
14										S₁			R₁	A₁	I₁
15															

Triple Word Score   Triple Letter Score

Double Word Score   Double Letter Score

| B₃ | D₂ | I₁ | N₁ | O₁ | O₁ | U₁ | 43   ★★

| A₁ | C₃ | E₁ | I₁ | R₁ | R₁ | T₁ | 108   ★★★

| G₂ | I₁ | O₁ | R₁ | S₁ | T₁ | T₁ | 229   ★★★★

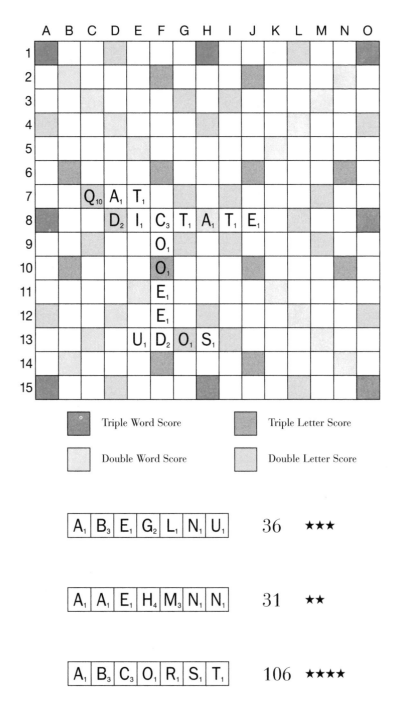

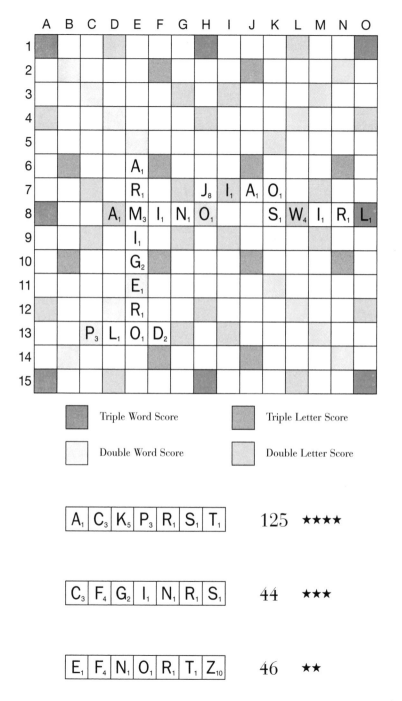

☆ 110

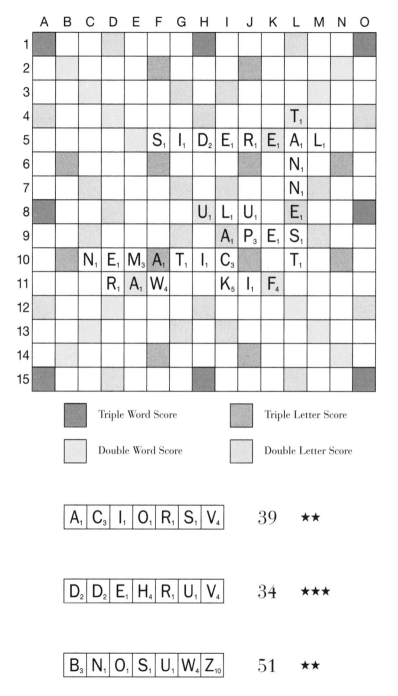

	A	B	C	D	E	F	G	H	I	J	K	L	M	N	O
1												T₁			
5						S₁	I₁	D₂	E₁	R₁	E₁	A₁	L₁		
6												N₁			
7												N₁			
8								U₁	L₁	U₁		E₁			
9									A₁	P₃	E₁	S₁			
10		N₁	E₁	M₃	A₁	T₁	I₁	C₃				T₁			
11		R₁	A₁	W₄				K₅	I₁	F₄					

Triple Word Score   Triple Letter Score

Double Word Score   Double Letter Score

A₁ C₃ I₁ O₁ R₁ S₁ V₄   39 ★★

D₂ D₂ E₁ H₄ R₁ U₁ V₄   34 ★★★

B₃ N₁ O₁ S₁ U₁ W₄ Z₁₀   51 ★★

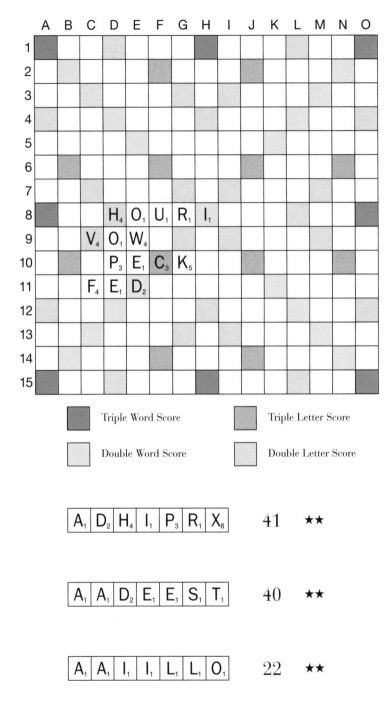

Triple Word Score

Triple Letter Score

Double Word Score

Double Letter Score

| D_2 | E_1 | I_1 | I_1 | L_1 | O_1 | Z_{10} |

99 ★★★

| D_2 | E_1 | I_1 | M_3 | O_1 | P_3 | U_1 |

37 ★★★

| A_1 | F_4 | L_1 | L_1 | O_1 | T_1 | Y_4 |

45 ★★★

| A₁ | D₂ | E₁ | F₄ | I₁ | R₁ | R₁ | 81 | ★★★ |

| A₁ | E₁ | G₂ | I₁ | N₁ | R₁ | U₁ | 52 | ★★★ |

| B₃ | I₁ | L₁ | M₃ | N₁ | T₁ | Y₄ | 29 | ★★★ |

	A	B	C	D	E	F	G	H	I	J	K	L	M	N	O
1				T₁	R₁	A₁	D₂			T₁	O₁	R₁	I₁		
2					W₄	E₁	N₁		R₁		A₁				
3					N₁			E₁		D₂					
4	B₃	U₁	R₁	N₁	O₁	U₁	T₁		A₁		I₁			
5	I₁					U₁		T₁	W₄	O₁				
6	N₁					R₁		Y₄	E₁					
7	E₁					E₁			A₁					
8			Q₁₀	U₁	E₁	S₁	T₁		V₄					
9	D₂	R₁	O₁	I₁	T₁		O₁	X₈	L₁	I₁	P₃			
10	I₁								N₁					
11	S₁							G₂						
12	H₄													
13														
14														
15														

Triple Word Score   Triple Letter Score

Double Word Score   Double Letter Score

B₃ K₅ O₁ O₁ S₁ Y₄ ☐   112 ★★★★

E₁ E₁ G₂ L₁ N₁ O₁ V₄   46 ★★

C₃ C₃ E₁ I₁ N₁ O₁ S₁   596 ★★★★

	A	B	C	D	E	F	G	H	I	J	K	L	M	N	O
1		T₁													
2		I₁			T₁										
3	P	E₁				O₁									
4	R₁			H₄	A₁	O₁									
5	E₁	N₁	T₁	A₁	I₁	L₁	E₁	R₁							
6	N₁							E₁							
7	T₁							B₃							
8	I₁			V₄	I₁	R₁	T₁	U₁	E₁						
9	C₃			A₁				S₁							
10	E₁			L₁											
11	S₁	O₁	L	I₁	D₂	I₁	F₄	Y₄							
12				D₂	E₁	F₄		A₁							
13								U₁							
14								L₁							
15								D₂							

Triple Word Score Triple Letter Score

Double Word Score Double Letter Score

B₃ E₁ L₁ M₃ R₁ R₁ Y₄   88   ★★★

E₁ E₁ G₂ P₃ S₁ T₁ Y₄   50   ★★★

A₁ H₄ I₁ P₃ P₃ S₁ T₁   253   ★★★★

Answers

7. FAX 7C 32
WOUNDING 5E 26
FJORD 2F 28

8. RECKONING 5G 66
PINUP 1H 27
FLAUNT 2J 34

9. PIT 3C 26
LEARN M2 29
PREEN 3C 38

10. EERIE O11 27
JUDO O7 39
QAT J6 35

11. FEARED 15D 58
MANAGER A8 36
MILDEW D10 43

12. TOAD 2G 22
WREN M2 25
CARHOP D1 37

13. BIZ C13 42
LEMUR C11 39
POOF 8L 48

14. JOINT F2 34
DIMPLY G4 33
UNKIND 8J 50

15. PALP 7F 36
ICILY 8K 39
EYELET L10 37

16. READMIT N2 105
THUMB 8K 48
GLORY N2 47

17. VICE 10B 35
UNAWARE O4 88
EJECT J9 35

18. IFS 7B 35
LINOLEUM 11D 90
THREW O7 41

19. DEHORN G7 34
DELIMIT 7C 30
EAGERER 4H 26

20. HAILER 6J 45
LIQUOR L3 32
JUBILEE D8 40

21. BOLOGNA 10H 29
ABOVE 1A 30
WHARF 6J 43

22. WIDOW 4H 44
PREFAB J6 33
APROPOS E5 44

23. FORK 7C 28
CHIEFLY E5 72
HEEHAW D3 30

24. WISE 14A 40
PHOBIA 15E 39
OVERALL O7 86

25. EVEN H1 33
DIRECT 2B 34
WONDERFUL 4F 84

26. VEX 14D 60
OUTDANCED H7 92
REVAMP C3 32

27. WAKER 10D 30
TANDEM A7 43
FACULTY E5 67

28. PRONTO D4 32
RELIEF D3 42
OKAPI 1K 48

29. NINJA A1 36
HAIKU C9 49
EBONY 2B 36

30. DETACH 4D 35
UPTOWN N2 52
RELAX C3 46

31. UNZIPS J2 38
OVUM 1A 36
HIPPIE 2J 42

32. IDLE 12A 32
ICE 4C 28
TARDY I4 34

33. DEPTH 2J 55
UNPAID 15J 36
ALIVE A1 39

34. COUGAR N10 35
MIXING 12J 56
BUGGY D8 29

35. GOPHER 8J 45
AHOY 13L 35
MENTAL 14F 37

36. AMEND 15D 49
RABID H11 38
JELLY D11 38

37. PARDON 12A 30
YOUNG H11 39
BRUTISH K5 48

38. ADMIT H11 30
UNCLASP N8 97
AWARE 12H 34

39. TOWEL 9G 41
BACON 6D 37
NAG 9G 28

40. GABLES 12A 39
DENIM 6B 39
SPHINX 12H 41

41. UNDONE H10 27
OPERA 8K 30
TWELVE 2I 42

42. BEAUT 11K 27
RESIFT L1 45
AMOUR 1A 43

43. MAGICAL 3C 35
ODDITY M2 39
OMEGA 14A 35

44. PAID 3K 29
EXPORT 9F 51
NEUTRINO O2 77

45. DOZES 10H 49
NYLON D1 40
ORATE B2 35

46. INDUCT H10 33
GLOAT 11D 25
GLITCH K1 24

47. YEARN K8 27
TABLEAU L2 83
HONEYMOON 8G 60

48. BIRCH 10F 40
CARIBOU K5 60
TWOFOLD 4I 32

49. TEPID E10 36
COPOUT 2J 44
EXTREME 3H 48

50. TEEM H1 42
IDIOM 1G 43
REDEFINE H8 48

51. AMBITION 6A 27
VANISH B1 53
FRESHER 11E 52

52. APPOINT 2I 48
OUTLAW 10E 36
QUIT 1A 83

53. BUS 10F 32
OBLIGATED 14A 80
TWENTY 13H 32

54. LABIA N10 41
RARITY B10 35
JINXING 8G 33

55. INVASION E1 76
ASYLUM 10I 41
UNWED E7 32

56. ENTITLE O4 84
BEHIND E2 56
HEADIER C7 47

57. PHOBIC C8 30
GHOST H11 39
MIAOW 8A 48

58. PUBLIC 1J 45
BRAVO O8 48
INHERENT 2H 69

59. ALOOF 15A 41
GROANING N2 74
KNOW 4I 43

60. MARROW 8J 33
EPITOME 2H 35
CURVY C3 34

61. HAVOC 1G 39
GOVERN H10 42
OUTROWED E4 48

62. UNFAIRER K5 44
ALBINO O10 44
HANG G3 39

63. FATAL K2 38
FORTES N1 48
MAILBOX 11E 36

64. HYPER L10 38
PLUSH M5 48
BALLGAME 14B 34

65. DUH M12 33
TIME J8 32
DETRACT E4 38

66. BONNY H11 30
KINGDOM M3 47
FRESH 14F 45

67. JINGLE O4 75
BOWLEG A3 42
FATHERLAND 15F 51

68. GRIEF 12C 31
TENSION M5 89
GROWL 12C 31

69. WHEREIN A3 39
GYP 2I 38
FELINE N10 47

70. BAA 13B 29
FISCAL 4H 42
BEGONE J6 37

71. BICEP 9A 23
WHEEZE 7E or 9E 50
DECORUM E5 48

72. CUBED E2 27
ARMBAND 5E 48
RAJ D10 49

73. INFOLD 5A 29
NEWFOUND H8 48
STEAK 10F 35

74. APLOMB D7 30
PERISH 10A 45
PENCHANT H8 57

75. SIXTH 10D 31
RUNDOWN A6 33
HORIZON A6 57

76. QUAINTEST 8G 57
EQUATORIAL 8F 110
LITHIUM 9F 90

77. GLOAM 5C 30
REMIND I5 34
REENTER L1 32

78. GURNEY L8 39
LADYBUGS H8 54
UNABLE A1 38

79. WOULD 2F 50
OUTFIT H1 39
RATIONAL C5 60

80. AUDIO 10J 34
HUMIDITY L6 49
NATIVES C3 33

81. PIVOTAL 1H 39
QAT 9M 31
UNJUST 2J 30

82. AYE D4 51
AMORALLY C1 78
RATATAT 3B 28

83. NITRIC L10 28
NINETY 10B 28
EMBARGO D3 34

84. ULTERIOR 14F 62
HATTER N10 57
ALOHA 3K 43

85. GALLON 4A 24
WIDGETS 11E 48
JEWELRY 13G 64

86. GHOUL H11 39
ZINNIA D1 50
BEDTIME L9 26

87. DWELT 1K 46
ABANDON 5E 40
JACUZZI 6F 60

88. MIRTH 6B 43
GHERKIN 6I 40
PETUNIA A4 27

89. POWERFUL 3F 34
SULK 11I 27
SUBLIME 5E 44

90. ANALYTIC H8 51
ANDROID 12D 74
PHLEGM 4D 36

91. ALMANAC 14I 79
SCYTHE L2 45
EPIDEMIC 4C 80

92. EXTEND 13H 44
BUNCHED 12D 38
ORNAMENT 5E 90

93. ERECTING H8 36
WESTWARD B2 30
VOICED H1 47

94. MOTH B7 37
ADJOURN 3B 32
WILDCAT E8 26

95. COZIEST 11E 72
OBSERVE 10F 31
OBOE 7G 27

96. BAYED 5K 37
COWBELL M7 36
MIXTURE L6 48

97. CIAO 9F 19
LAWNMOWER 8G 54
WELFARE 9C 80

98. ROUNDUP D4 20
HOPED 7F 31
IGNITION E5 86

99. DISLIKE 13A 86
INVOICE E5 48
PILAF B10 46

100. ADZ 13A 62
ADORATION J1 66
MAJESTIC 1H 101

101. DODO K11 25
CURTAIN 11E 36
JOURNAL 12F 30

102. FRUITY L3 24
FOUNDER K5 44
ALMOND H10 38

103. ANCHORMEN 4D
114
MASKED 12I 49
SPHINX C2 71

104. TOWAGE N1 50
AIRSTRIKE 5E 82
JULEP D1 48

105. BANDWAGON 10F
37
BUOYANT E5 48
LOOPY C2 39

106. SQUADRON 13C 92
ZENITH 2J 76
WHATCHAMACALLIT
O1 96

107. UNBID 15K 43
REDIRECT A1 108
GASTROENTERITIS O1
229

108. NEBULAE 11E 36
ANTHEM G6 31
BROADCAST D4 106

109. JOCKSTRAP H7 125
CROSSING K5 44
FROZEN D1 46

110. MYALGIA 5E 52
IRKSOME 2H 46
LOYALIST 5D 47

Hints

I've defined several types of hints, based upon the bonus squares a play covers, the number of letters in the word, how many overlapping words are formed simultaneously, etc. The following abbreviations will serve as hints.

DLS: Double Letter Score

DWS: Double Word Score

TLS: Triple Letter Score

TWS: Triple Word Score

B: Bingo, meaning all seven tiles are used.

9+: Nine-letter answer word or longer

O(n): Overlapping parallel play, meaning the play is made parallel to another play, where "n" is the number of letters that overlap and form additional words. Only words that overlap two or more letters will show that hint.

E: Extension play, meaning the letters added to the board extend a word already on the board.

Scoring Hints

The scores can give you insights as to which bonus squares the answer is played on and how many letters the solution word contains. For example, a score divisible by 3, such as 39, might signify that the answer will cover a TWS and that the letters (including any DLS squares bonuses) will sum to 13. Or, if the total is *not* divisible by 2, then you know that the answer won't be a simple DWS without some additional parallel play score, because DWS word scores *must* be divisible by 2. Non-bingos that total 50 points or more will usually include either a DLS-TWS or TLS-DWS combination or use a J, Q, X, or Z on a bonus square. The location of bingos may often be deduced by subtracting 50 from the total and examining that number. If it's divisible by 3, there's a reasonable chance the word will cover a TWS. There are other scoring deductions easily made, but we leave them for you to discover.

Parallel Plays

After over 20 years of teaching the game, I believe that the single most transformational skill a player can attain is learning how to look at the board in order to find parallel plays. To illustrate: I've occasionally taught daylong classes that include learning all 101 two-letter words and how to use them effectively, how to find seven- and eight-letter words with ease, how to balance your rack and keep the most bingo-prone tiles, and how to think strategically when confronted with several reasonable choices for plays. Before taking the class, many of the students are only familiar with making plays perpendicular to other words. After the class, I often receive feedback from some students (via e-mail these days) that usually goes something like this, to paraphrase: "I never realized how much more interesting and fun the game is after learning how to make parallel plays. It's like night and day. The game becomes so much more engrossing and I have so many more choices every play."

Given that, I *urge* you to refer to the list of two-letter words repeatedly until you learn them by heart. Your scoring will very likely improve by 50 points or more per game just by knowing and finding those parallel plays. You may think that the "setup" puzzles in this book only happen in a book. I'm here to say that *every game* has such plays if only you develop the skills to see them. This book is an attempt to give you oodles of practice in looking for just such plays. And, for the record, almost every diagram in this book came from a real game against Quackle, the "king" of SCRABBLE game-playing software, created by

John O'Laughlin and Jason Katz-Brown, though some required minor adjustments to ensure the quality of the puzzles.

Finding Bingos

People inexperienced at finding seven- and eight-letter words may be surprised to learn that it's not all that difficult to learn how to find them with but a few clues. The main skill is to learn the common beginnings and endings of these longer words. For instance, given AINOOTV, if you knew the seven-letter word ended in –TION, it might not take long to find the word.

In order to help you gain this skill, we're presenting below common beginnings and endings for bingos.

Beginnings: ANTI-, BE-, DE-, DIS-, EN-, EX-, IN-, OUT-, OVER-, PRE-, RE-, UN-

Endings: -ABLE, -AGE, -AL, -ARD, -ARY, -ATE, -ED, -EE, -ENCE, -ENE, -ER, -ERY, -FUL, -IAN(S), -IC, -IDE, -IER, -IEST, -INE, -ING, -ION, -ISH, -ITY, -LAND, -LIKE, -LY, -OID, -OMY, -ON, -OUR, -OUS, -SHIP, -STY, -TUDE, -URE(S)

Note that there are many more beginnings and endings. For a more thorough list, see the revised edition of *Everything SCRABBLE*.

7. Top: DLS, O2
Middle: DWS, E
Bottom: TLS-TLS

8. Top: B, 9+, E
Middle: TWS
Bottom: TLS-DWS

9. Top: DWS, O3
Middle: DWS, O5
Bottom: DLS-DWS, O4

10. Top: DLS-TWS, O3
Middle: TWS
Bottom: TLS

11. Top: DLS-TWS, O3
Middle: DLS-TWS
Bottom: DLS-DWS, O3

12. Top: TLS, O3
Middle: DWS, O3
Bottom: DLS-DWS

13. Top: DWS
Middle: DWS,O3
Bottom: DLS-TWS

14. Top: TLS-TLS
Middle: DLS-DLS
Bottom: DLS-TWS

15. Top: DLS-DLS, O4
Middle: DLS-TWS
Bottom: DLS-DWS, O4

16. Top: TLS-DWS, B, O3
Middle: DLS-TWS
Bottom: TLS-DWS

17. Top: TLS, O2
Middle: DLS-TWS, B, O2
Bottom: TLS

18. Top: DLS, O3
Middle: DWS-DWS, B
Bottom: TWS, O2

19. Top: DLS-DLS, O2
Middle: DLS-DLS-DLS,
O3, E
Bottom: DLS-DWS, O3

20. Top: TLS-TLS, O3
Middle: DLS-DWS
Bottom: DWS

21. Top: TLS-TLS, O2
Middle: TWS
Bottom: TLS-TLS

22. Top: DLS-DWS
Middle: TLS-TLS, O2
Bottom: DWS-DWS

23. Top: DLS, O3
Middle: DWS-DWS
Bottom: DWS

24. Top: DWS, O3
Middle: TWS
Bottom: DLS-TWS, B

25. Top: DLS-TWS, O2
Middle: TLS-DWS
Bottom: DLS-DWS, B, 9+,
E

26. Top: TLS, O2
Middle: DLS-TWS, B, 9+,
E
Bottom: DLS-DWS

27. Top: TLS
Middle: DLS-TWS
Bottom: DWS-DWS

28. Top: DLS-DWS, O4
Middle: DLS-DWS, O3
Bottom: DLS-TWS

29. Top: TWS
Middle: DLS-DWS, O4
Bottom: TLS-DWS

30. Top: DWS, O3
Middle: TLS-DWS
Bottom: DLS-DWS

31. Top: TLS-TLS
Middle: DLS-TWS
Bottom: TLS-DWS

32. Top: DWS, O3
Middle: DWS, O3
Bottom: DLS, O5

33. Top: TLS-DWS, O3
Middle: DLS-TWS
Bottom: DLS-TWS

34. Top: TLS-DWS
Middle: DLS-DWS, O2
Bottom: DWS

35. Top: DLS-TWS
Middle: DWS, O3
Bottom: TLS-TLS, O4

36. Top: DLS-TWS, O5
Middle: DLS-TWS, O3
Bottom: DLS-DWS

37. Top: DLS-DWS, O2
Middle: DLS-TWS
Bottom: DWS-DWS

38. Top: DLS-TWS
Middle: TLS-DWS, B
Bottom: DLS-DWS, O4

39. Top: DLS-DLS, O4
Middle: TLS, O3
Bottom: DLS-DLS, O3

DLS = Double Letter Score; DWS = Double Word Score; TLS = Triple Letter Score;
TWS = Triple Word Score; B = Bingo; 9+ = Nine-letter word or longer;
O(n) = Overlapping parallel play of n letters; E = Extension play

40. Top: DLS-DWS, O2
Middle: TLS-TLS, O2
Bottom: DWS

41. Top: DLS-TWS
Middle: DLS-TWS
Bottom: TLS-DWS

42. Top: DWS, O3
Middle: DLS-DWS, O3, E
Bottom: DLS-TWS, O5

43. Top: DLS-DLS-DWS
Middle: DLS-DWS
Bottom: DWS, O3

44. Top: DWS, O3
Middle: DLS-DLS, O3
Bottom: DLS-TWS, B

45. Top: TLS, O2
Middle: DLS-DWS, O4
Bottom: TLS-DWS, O5

46. Top: DLS-TWS
Middle: DWS, O2
Bottom: DWS

47. Top: DWS
Middle: DLS-DWS, B, O2
Bottom: DLS-TWS, 9+, E

48. Top: TLS-TLS, O2
Middle: DWS-DWS, O3
Bottom: DLS-DWS

49. Top: DWS, O2
Middle: TLS-DWS
Bottom: DLS-DWS

50. Top: DLS-TWS, O3
Middle: TWS, O4
Bottom: DLS-TWS, E

51. Top: TLS-TLS
Middle: TLS-DWS
Bottom: DWS-DWS

52. Top: TLS-DWS, O3
Middle: TLS-TLS, O2
Bottom: DLS-TWS, O4

53. Top: TLS, O3
Middle: TLS-DWS, B, 9+
Bottom: DLS-DWS

54. Top: TLS-DWS, O4
Middle: TLS-DWS
Bottom: O2, E

55. Top: DWS, B
Middle: TLS-TLS
Bottom: DWS, O3

56. Top: DLS-TWS, B, O3
Middle: DWS, O4
Bottom: DLS-DWS, O4

57. Top: DWS
Middle: DLS-TWS
Bottom: DLS-TWS, O4

58. Top: DLS-TWS
Middle: DLS-TWS
Bottom: TLS, B

59. Top: DLS-TWS, O4
Middle: TLS-DWS, B
Bottom: DWS, O4

60. Top: TWS
Middle: TLS-DWS, O2
Bottom: DLS-DWS

61. Top: TWS
Middle: DLS-TWS
Bottom: DWS-DWS, E

62. Top: DWS-DWS, E
Middle: DLS-TWS
Bottom: DLS, O4

63. Top: DWS, O3
Middle: TLS-DWS, O5
Bottom: DWS

64. Top: DWS
Middle: DLS-DLS, O3
Bottom: TLS-DWS, E

65. Top: DWS, O3
Middle: TLS, O3
Bottom: DWS, O2

66. Top: TWS, E
Middle: DLS-DLS-DWS
Bottom: TLS-TLS, O3

67. Top: DLS-TWS
Middle: DLS-TWS
Bottom: TWS, 9+, E

68. Top: DWS, O3
Middle: DLS-DLS, B, O6
Bottom: DWS, O3

69. Top: TWS
Middle: TLS, O2
Bottom: TLS-DWS

70. Top: DWS, O3
Middle: DLS-DWS
Bottom: TLS-TLS, O5

71. Top: DLS, O2
Middle: DLS-DLS, O4
Bottom: DWS-DWS

72. Top: DWS, O2
Middle: DWS-DWS
Bottom: DWS, O3

73. Top: DWS
Middle: DLS-TWS, E
Bottom: TLS-TLS, O3

74. Top: DLS-DWS
Middle: TLS-TLS, O5
Bottom: DLS-TWS, E

75. Top: TLS
Middle: TWS
Bottom: TWS

76. Top: DLS-TWS, 9+, E
Middle: DLS-TWS, B, 9+,
E
Bottom: DLS-DLS, B, O3

77. Top: DWS, O3
Middle: DLS-DLS, O3
Bottom: DLS-DWS, O3

78. Top: DLS-DWS
Middle: DLS-TWS, E
Bottom: DLS-TWS

79. Top: TLS-TLS
Middle: DLS-TWS, E
Bottom: DLS-DLS, B

80. Top: TLS-TLS, O4
Middle: DWS, E
Bottom: DLS-DLS-DWS

81. Top: DLS-TWS
Middle: DLS
Bottom: TLS-DWS

82. Top: DWS, O3
Middle: DLS-DWS, B
Bottom: DLS-DWS, O3

83. Top: DLS-DWS
Middle: TLS-TLS, O3
Bottom: DLS-DWS

84. Top: TLS-TLS, B
Middle: TLS-DWS, O5
Bottom: DWS, O3

85. Top: DLS-DWS, O2
Middle: DWS-DWS
Bottom: DLS-DLS-DWS

86. Top: DLS-TWS
Middle: DLS-DWS
Bottom: DLS-DWS, E

87. Top: DLS-TWS
Middle: DWS-DWS
Bottom: TLS-TLS

88. Top: TLS-TLS, O2
Middle: TLS-TLS, O2
Bottom: TWS,

89. Top: DLS-DWS, E
Middle: DWS
Bottom: DWS-DWS

90. Top: DLS-TWS, E
Middle: DLS-DWS, B
Bottom: DLS-DWS

91. Top: TLS-DWS, B
Middle: DWS, O3
Bottom: DLS-DWS, B

92. Top: DLS-DWS
Middle: DLS-DWS
Bottom: DWS-DWS, B

93. Top: DLS-TWS, E
Middle: DWS
Bottom: TWS

94. Top: TLS, O3
Middle: DLS-DWS
Bottom: DWS

95. Top: DWS-DWS
Middle: TLS, O3
Bottom: DLS-DLS, O3

96. Top: DWS, O2
Middle: DLS-DWS
Bottom: DLS-DWS, E

97. Top: DLS-DLS, O3
Middle: DLS-TWS, 9+, E
Bottom: DLS-DLS-DLS, B,
O3

98. Top: DWS
Middle: DLS-DLS, O5
Bottom: DWS-DWS, B

99. Top: DLS-DWS, B
Middle: DWS-DWS
Bottom: TLS-DWS, O3

100. Top: DWS, O3
Middle: TLS-TLS, B, 9+, E
Bottom: DLS-TWS, B

101. Top: DWS, O4
Middle: DWS-DWS
Bottom: DLS-DWS

102. Top: DWS
Middle: DWS-DWS
Bottom: DLS-TWS

103. Top: DWS-DWS, B,
9+, E
Middle: DWS, O5
Bottom: DLS-DWS, O2

104. Top: TLS-DWS, O5
Middle: DWS, B, 9+
Bottom: DLS-DWS

105. Top: TLS-TLS, 9+,
O2, E
Middle: DWS-DWS, E
Bottom: DWS, O5

106. Top: DLS-DLS-DWS,
B
Middle: TLS-DWS
Bottom: TWS, 9+, O2, E

107. Top: DLS-TWS, O3
Middle: DLS-TWS-TWS, E
Bottom: DLS-DLS-TWS-
TWS, B, 9+, O3, E

DLS = Double Letter Score; DWS = Double Word Score; TLS = Triple Letter Score;
TWS = Triple Word Score; B = Bingo; 9+ = Nine-letter word or longer;
O(n) = Overlapping parallel play of n letters; E = Extension play

108. Top: DWS-DWS
Middle: DLS-DLS, O3
Bottom: DWS-DWS, B, 9+,
E

109. Top: DLS-TWS, B,
9+, E
Middle: DWS-DWS, E
Bottom: DLS-DWS

110. Top: DWS-DWS
Middle: TLS-DWS
Bottom: DWS-DWS

111. Top: DLS-DWS, O2
Middle: DLS-DWS
Bottom: DLS-TWS

112. Top: DWS, O2
Middle: DLS-TWS
Bottom: DWS, E

113. Top: DLS-DWS, B,
O5
Middle: DLS, O5
Bottom: DLS-DLS-DWS

114. Top: DLS-DLS, B, O2
Middle: DWS-DWS, 9+, E
Bottom: DWS, E

115. Top: DLS-TWS, B,
9+, E
Middle: DLS-TWS, O2
Bottom: TWS-TWS-TWS,
B, 9+, E

116. Top: DLS-DLS-DWS,
B
Middle: DLS-TWS
Bottom: DLS-TWS-TWS,
9+, O2, E

DLS = Double Letter Score; DWS = Double Word Score; TLS = Triple Letter Score;
TWS = Triple Word Score; B = Bingo; 9+ = Nine-letter word or longer;
O(n) = Overlapping parallel play of n letters; E = Extension play

Important Short Words

Below in bold are the 101 allowable two-letter words. The letters to the left of the words can precede them, and the ones to the right can follow them to make three-letter words. So B can come before AA to make BAA, and H, L, and S can follow it to make AAH, AAL, and AAS. Memorizing this list will improve your SCRABBLE scores.

Before	Word	After
B	**AA**	HLS
CDFGJKLNSTW	**AB**	ASY
BCDFGHLMPRSTW	**AD**	DOSZ
GHKMNSTW	**AE**	
BDFGHJLMNRSTWYZ	**AG**	AEOS
ABDHNPRY	**AH**	AIS
R	**AI**	DLMNRST
ABDGPS	**AL**	ABELPST
BCDGHJLNPRTY	**AM**	AIPU
BCDFGMNPRTVW	**AN**	ADEITY
BCEFGJLMOPTVWY	**AR**	BCEFKMST
ABFGHKLMPRTVWZ	**AS**	HKPS
BCEFGHKLMOPQRSTVW	**AT**	ET
CDHJLMNPRSTVWY	**AW**	AELN
FLMPRSTWZ	**AX**	E
BCDFGHJKLMNPRSWY	**AY**	ES
AO	**BA**	ADGHLMNPRSTY
O	**BE**	DEGLNSTY
O	**BI**	BDGNOSTZ
	BO	ABDGOPSTWXY
A	**BY**	ES
O	**DE**	BEFLNVWXY
AU	**DO**	CEGLMNRSTW
BFGLMPRTWZ	**ED**	HS
DKR	**EF**	FST
FHPY	**EH**	
BCDEGMST	**EL**	DFKLMS
FGHMR	**EM**	ESU
BDFGHKMPSTWY	**EN**	DGS
FHPS	**ER**	AEGNRS
BFHOPRY	**ES**	S
BFGHJLMNPRSTVWY	**ET**	AH
DHKLRSV	**EX**	
	FA	BDGNRSTXY
	FE	DEHMNRSTUWYZ
AE	**GO**	ABDORSTX
ASW	**HA**	DEGHJMOPSTWY
ST	**HE**	HMNPRSTWXY
ACGKP	**HI**	CDEMNPST
O	**HM**	M
MORTW	**HO**	BDEGNPTWY
ABDFGHKLMRV	**ID**	S
DKR	**IF**	FS
ABDFGHJKLPRSTWYZ	**IN**	KNS
ABCDHKLMPQSTVWX	**IS**	M
ABDFGHKLNPSTWX	**IT**	S
	JO	BEGTWY
OS	**KA**	BEFSTY
S	**KI**	DFNPRST
A	**LA**	BCDGMPRSTVWXY
	LI	BDENPST

Before	Word	After
	LO	BGOPTWX
A	**MA**	CDEGNPRSTWXY
E	**ME**	DGLMNTW
A	**MI**	BCDGLMRSX
HU	**MM**	
	MO	ABCDGLMNOPRSTW
AE	**MU**	DGMNST
	MY	C
A	**NA**	BEGHMNPWY
AO	**NE**	BEGTW
O	**NO**	BDGHMORSTW
G	**NU**	BNST
BCGHMNPRSTY	**OD**	ADES
DFHJRTVW	**OE**	S
	OF	FT
FNOP	**OH**	MOS
KP	**OI**	L
DMNRSTY	**OM**	S
CDEFHIMSTWY	**ON**	EOS
BCFHKLMPST	**OP**	EST
CDFGKMNT	**OR**	ABCEST
BCDGKMNSW	**OS**	E
BCDHJLMNPRSTVWY	**OW**	ELN
BCFGLPSV	**OX**	OY
BCFHJST	**OY**	
S	**PA**	CDHLMNPRSTWXY
AO	**PE**	ACDEGHNPRSTW
	PI	ACEGNPSTUX
	QI	S
AEIO	**RE**	BCDEFGIMPSTVX
A	**SH**	AEHY
P	**SI**	BCMNPRSTX
	SO	BDLMNPSTUWXY
EU	**TA**	BDEGJMNOPRSTUVWX
	TI	CELNPST
	TO	DEGMNOPRTWY
DH	**UH**	
BCGHLMRSVY	**UM**	MP
BDFGHJMNPRST	**UN**	S
CDHPSTY	**UP**	OS
BJMNP	**US**	E
BCGHJMNOPRT	**UT**	AES
AEO	**WE**	BDENT
T	**WO**	EKNOSTW
	XI	S
	XU	
PR	**YA**	GHKMPRWY
ABDEKLPRTW	**YE**	AHNPSTW
	YO	BDKMNUW
	ZA	GPSX